ADVANCE PRAISE FOR *LIBERATING THE SELF*

"This exceptional book combines penetrating psychological analysis with profound spiritual wisdom. Stephen is with you on each page, warmly encouraging, with stories and practical suggestions, always clear and so very helpful."

—**RICK HANSON**

PhD, author of *Buddha's Brain* and *Neurodharma*

"Stephen writes with a rare clarity and precision about Awakening and the path to realization in this life. If you are looking for a profound guide to using reflection, meditation, and wisdom to awaken, I highly recommend this book."

—**MARK COLEMAN**

Cofounder of the Mindfulness Training Institute, author of *From Suffering to Peace*

"As Buddhism deepens in the West, there is concern over the gap between Awakening and problematic conditioned behavior. Stephen offers concrete tools to ward off spiritual bypassing and more fully liberate the self."

—**KATHERINE DAIKI SENSHIN GRIFFITH**

Sensei, head teacher of the Zen Center of Los Angeles

"*Liberating the Self* describes a Zen life by someone who has genuinely walked the way, enriched by insights ranging from the Theravada to modern psychology. A unique and worthy contribution to contemporary Zen literature."

—**JAMES ISHMAEL FORD**

Author of *The Intimate Way of Zen*

"Stephen's splendid book gives us a comprehensive roadmap for practice. When guided by an experienced teacher, the extraordinary ordinariness of Zen life can truly be realized."
—PAUL GYODO AGOSTINELLI
Sensei, founder of the Eon Zen Center

"A warm and pragmatic guide for turning even our most challenging experiences into opportunities for Awakening. Highly recommended for practitioners looking to deepen their practice."
—DAVE CUOMO
Head of practice at the Angel City Zen Center

"In *Liberating the Self*, Stephen has provided an invaluable guide for what lies beyond First Awakening. It will be of immense benefit to those on the path."
—STEPHEN JAMES PIGOTT,
Educator, host of the *Guru Viking Podcast*

"A must-read for both beginner and advanced practitioners that combines psychological acumen with insights from profound realization. Stephen's kind heart shines through every page."
—LIAM MYOSHIN MONTANARELLI,
PhD, LCSW-C, psychotherapist

"I've witnessed firsthand through personal practice and professional observation the power of the practices contained in this book. The destination is no other place than freedom."
—DEREK MCCLURE,
Licensed mental health counselor, Dharma practitioner

LIBERATING THE SELF

LIBERATING
the *Self*

Buddhist Practices for an
Authentic Life

Stephen Snyder

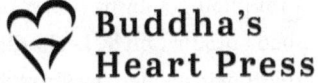
Buddha's
Heart Press

Buddha's Heart Press
awakeningdharma.org
Midland, MI, USA

Library of Congress Control Number: 2024918441

ISBN: 979-8-9881720-1-7 (paperback)
ISBN: 979-8-9881720-2-4 (e-book)

Editing by Erin Parker
Copyediting by Julia Grandison
Proofreading by Lynn Slobogian
Illustrations by Samuel Quinn
Cover and interior design by Jazmin Welch (fleck creative studio)
Cover photography by Ivana Cajina via Unsplash
E-book production by Legible Publishing Services
Project management by Carra Simpson

I dedicate this book to the future teachers of Awakening Dharma. May they carry on the important work of deep realization and openhearted living while orienting toward greater authenticity.

CONTENTS

FOREWORD

In *Liberating the Self*, Stephen Mugen Snyder, one of the most deeply experienced spiritual teachers in contemporary Buddhism, has produced a masterwork, one that is devoted to helping each of us realize our true nature and, in so doing, find inner freedom and peace of mind. Mugen understands intimately the journey that each of us must take to heal ourselves of our mental and emotional ailments and find the peace we want to be. Speaking with honesty about his own journey and with sincere concern for the struggles of others, Mugen has created a pathway of specific practices to help each of us transform our negative emotions into kindness and compassion for ourselves and others. Underlying all of this is the working of the Absolute and the profound spiritual experience that is the hallmark of Buddhist practice and teaching.

This book directly acquaints us with the ways in which we find ourselves living with psychological dysfunction, described here as our "core wound," and why we remain unable to overcome it. Mugen then introduces a practice of introspection to locate the sense of weakness or failure associated with the core wound. From there, the investigation deepens to recognize that our inner experience also contains a place of peace that can be accessed at any time. This place is our innate goodness, endowed to us by the Absolute from which all joy and happiness flows. It is in this discovery that the journey of transformation begins and never ends.

Mugen guides us in detail through the great distortions of hatred, anger, weakness and insecurity, envy and jealousy, guilt, greed and resentment, and cruelty. In each section, we learn to release our core deficiency and, by doing so, allow our true, holistic nature to emerge. In this way, hatred gives way to peace, envy to joy, guilt to loving- kindness. The time spent in this work is vital to releasing the grip of our belief in our existence as a self separate from others.

Moving to the heart of the matter, Mugen provides an extensive course of practice for liberating us from the very notion of a separate self and encountering the transcendent experience of the Absolute. This opening to the Absolute requires completely letting go of fixed ideas about ourselves and others and really trusting our heart and spirit. It is here that the moving testimony of Mugen's students is most helpful. These are people drawn from all walks of life who have experienced extraordinary life-altering encounters with the Absolute by practicing the teachings found in this book. The result of these *kenshō*, or Awakenings, is reverence for the miracle of this world and our life while remaining ready at all times to answer the call of service to others.

Mugen, master that he is, will be the first to say that he is simply pointing the way. It is you who must take the next step to make these teachings your own. And when you do, please pass them on to others. After all, this life of peace and joy belongs to all of us. Don't hesitate. Please turn the page and begin . . .

—MARK SANDO MININBERG, ROSHI

INTRODUCTION

SHAKYAMUNI BUDDHA DAIOSHO is held in the highest regard by Buddhists worldwide. For many, he is the personification of realized perfection. He is held as a human who dispenses wise meditation and practical spiritual advice, while not having the normal foibles of ordinary humans. This has led some Buddhist teachers, in their teaching, to unknowingly disregard the work of purifying and releasing the building blocks of the sense of self. In fact, on the spiritual path of Awakening, we all, and each, need to work our personality, our psychological material, and our identity beliefs. We need to candidly explore and sincerely question the rooted beliefs and cherished conceptual convictions about ourselves and the world we inhabit. We must repeatedly examine everything around us, as if we are holding up an inner compass that reveals what is ultimately true.

This personality work is crucial at many points on our spiritual journey, both before and after Awakening. I learned this lesson personally, as I share in the introduction to my book *Demystifying Awakening*:

> I felt my conceptual foundation shift in those moments of First Awakening. I was not me anymore. There was a deep knowing that I would never again believe the illusion that we were each a me separate and distinct from every other me, every other life-form. I was free from being anchored to my conceptual me. I was tasting pure freedom. [. . .]
>
> I erroneously concluded this was going to be my permanent inner experience or state. My enthusiasm for this new reality overshadowed my habits of mind. Despite this deep realization, the structures of the self, of the me, were still in place and operating at reduced power. I did not know then that the next arduous step would be observing my behavior to identify what was incongruent with this realization and committing to investigate and engage with these discordant actions and behaviors. I did not fully grasp then that harmonizing my thoughts, behaviors, and actions with realizations experienced would be an ongoing lifetime endeavor. I see now there is no end to realizations nor personal work liberating habits of mind and behavior.

This is true for everyone in a First Awakening. A few weeks to months after experiencing either Awakening (*kenshō*) or Cessation, we return more fully to our personality workings. We leave the vast breathtaking Absence (emptiness) and enticing Presence (Beingness and love), and we return to the world dominated and dictated by personality perspectives. Our psychological neediness and what I call our "core wound" routinely flare up, demanding our undivided attention and allegiance.

For me, as a Sōtō Zen, Rinzai Zen, and Theravada Buddhist teacher, to confirm an Awakening I am looking for three components. First, a deep experience of no-self, which I call "absence of self." This is the perceived transparency or absence of the customary sense of self. Then there needs to be a deep unity experience, an experience of being an undivided part of the entire fabric of love of the Absolute. Finally, there needs to be a throughgoing recognition that these two components are truly who I am in the deepest reality.

A Cessation experience is the chief Awakening experience in the Theravada Buddhist tradition. This is a very deep, completely immersive experience. All of the ways we know ourselves, all mentality, and all materiality cease in the experience of Cessation. Cessation is the immense power of profound peace, the deepest stillness, and the fullness of Absence.

Some linger hesitatingly on the cusp of deep Awakening or Cessation, not fully letting go into the unbounded, uncontrolled free fall that characterizes deep realization. While waiting patiently for the revealing of the experiential depths of the Absolute, we want to take this time to rigorously question the conceptual convictions about who and what we are. This will prepare us more fully to release all perception of a me as we open to the Absolute Awakening itself.

> *I have written this book for all these practitioners whose personality material aches for deep exploration, thorough investigation, and original liberation.*

I have written this book for all these practitioners whose personality material aches for deep exploration, thorough investigation, and original liberation. *Liberating the Self* is designed as a continuation of *Demystifying Awakening*. In *Demystifying Awakening* I provide the maps of Awakening of both the Theravada and Zen Buddhist traditions. I also offer meditation and spiritual practices that are beneficial pre- and post-Awakening. In this book I focus on the sense of self, both on the organization of the concept of me and on practices to address and convert difficult emotions from expressions of identity to their source as authentic expression of the Absolute, the source of all manifestation and creation.

No First Awakening experience completely transforms our belief in our sense of self. Some parts of the self will be thoroughly seen through and converted to the direct functioning of the Absolute. For the parts of the self that remain held in place by our deep belief in the concept of me, we can employ the practices of this book to carefully and deliberately release the conceptual convictions in the me, allowing the purity of the Absolute to shine through, enlivening our behaviors. Liberating the self is an ongoing engagement that requires diligence, openheartedness, and ideally a skilled teacher to support and guide the student through these swirling waters of self.

To more fully engage and liberate the sense of self, we need to understand how the self is constructed and be able to recognize psychological patterns of personality we all share, so let us start there.

The Construction of Our Customary Sense of Self

We are born into a state of understanding that some in psychology refer to as "dual unity." Dual unity means we, as infants, perceive the world as a unity, an undivided Oneness. Yet this Oneness is functioning as a duality of infant and caregiver.

Our hunger needs as infants are fulfilled through being provided breast milk or formula. The resolution of our immediate hunger appears spontaneously and confirms the unity perception of the infant. In time, when our hunger and other needs for affection are not immediately met, we see that there is a separation, a gap of time and space, between our felt bodily need and its satisfaction or resolution. This begins the breakdown of the dual unity as the infant enters and joins the customary human perspective of duality—a clear separation between infant and caregiver. The infant begins to hold the view that hunger is within and satisfaction of hunger comes from without.

In this process of separation, of establishing our individuation as humans in the world, we turn away from the unity of the Absolute's Presence and love. We sense as developing humans that if we are to live, we must have the unrestricted support of our caregivers, birth families, and society.

While in dual unity, we elect at a critical point in our individuation development, we affirmatively choose, to turn away from the Oneness of Presence as our core identity. The separation of our developing sense of self and the Absolute's Presence creates a felt sense of a gap, a distance between us and the source, the Absolute reality. This growing gap inherent in the separation feels like a loss, a kind of crushing bodily felt failure. Because we must be heavily invested in maintaining beneficial relationships with our caregivers and birth family, we turn away from the Absolute's Presence. We reject the Absolute to be a viable member of our family, culture, and society.

This rejection of the Absolute is internalized for many of us as our crushing, abject failure, an unshakable confirmation that we are irreparably flawed and unfixable. I call this core egoic deficiency the "core wound."

This core wound is that inner experience of instability or perception of weakness often found in the solar plexus area of our body. Because of the core wound's longevity and the perception that it cannot be fixed, most of us make the only perceivable choice, which is to hide it from ourselves and others.

> *Personality is comprised of how we perceive ourselves, how others have historically mirrored how we are seen, and the judgmental mix of the two.*

We begin to create a personality to distract ourselves and others from the core wound. Personality is comprised of how we perceive ourselves, how others have historically mirrored how we are seen, and the judgmental mix of the two. One of the main functions of the personality is to direct all attention, including our own perception, away from the core wound.

There is a direct relationship between how much appropriate attention and attuned love we received from our caregivers and how large we feel the core wound to be. In other words, if we do not receive enough attuned love from caregivers, we are more likely to perceive the core wound and its accompanying discomfort and dis-ease as foundational.

When we bring our core wound and the accompanying psychological structures to the forefront of awareness, they cease to operate unseen. Through direct investigation, we can begin to understand each structure and advance it to present time, so that it can be matched more closely with our level of realization.

Good, Pure, Innocent One

One deep-set psychological structure can be called "the good, pure, innocent one," which arises in the face of the utterly unlimited power our caregivers have when we are quite young. We learn to recognize that the hunger, the neediness, is always within us. The solution, the satisfaction, is nearly always from the outside, from the other person, the big person, the adult. This survival imbalance results in our viewing our caregivers as godlike. Our survival, our very life, depends on them committing to taking care of us.

Because we have such an acute need for survival, we quickly learn we cannot respond to our caregiver with any assertion of power. The few times we might assert ourselves, we learn the power imbalance is too great a gulf for us to bridge. We submit to their power and authority in order to live.

As a result of our conclusion that the caregiver has the actual power of life and death, many of us transfer our own power and authority onto the caregiver. This leaves us feeling even smaller and increasingly vulnerable, incapable of hurting others or having suspect motives in our actions.

We allow this feeling to settle into our psyche. We come to believe, *I am the good one, the little innocent one, the pure one. I can do no wrong—ever! The adults have all the power, all the strength. They hold all the power over me.*

This conclusion allows us to survive childhood, yet by splitting off our power and strength, the structure can create problems for us as adults. When we are tracking and examining our behavior, we will have difficulty seeing our improper motivations or unskillful actions if we are still somewhat landed in the good, pure, innocent one identity. We repeatedly ask the question, *How could I intend to harm or hurt the other person with my words when I am always pure, good, and innocent?* This leaves us with a gap between our conduct and the accurate, objective view of our behavior. In other words, it makes it near impossible to see our missteps in life.

The good, pure, innocent one self-identity structure slows or prevents our changing.

This is not the only way that the good, pure, innocent one veils perception. We see ourselves and the world around us through this lens of identity. We witness others in our world taking action that we know is wrong, or that does not benefit us directly, and we cannot find a voice to object. This leads to feelings of impotent loss. We think, *If only I had some power or strength, I would stand up to the others and make my needs known.*

The good, pure, innocent one self-identity structure slows or prevents our changing. We may feel we are incapable and lacking the strength and power to fully engage our life or make deep, needed changes to our beliefs, behaviors, and personality structuring.

Superego

The identity structure of the inner critic or superego begins to form in the two- to five-year-old stage of development. We are learning to separate, individuate, from our caregivers. We leave the caregiver's side yet either keep them in view or know they are just around the corner, out of sight. When we feel upset or scared, we quickly race to once again see or touch our caregiver, confirming their availability should we be in need.

At some point we take the next step and begin to create an internalized caregiver, which is the superego. In this way we always have our caregiver close at hand. When we need to soothe our angst, we can connect to the caregiver within.

Unexpectedly, we also imbue this internalized caregiver with our power and judgment. The superego then begins to function primarily as a critic of our behavior and actions. Particularly when we make a mistake or do something wrong, our internalized caregiver reacts with a quick negative judgment. We internally hear things like "You did that wrong!" or "You are the stupidest person!"

Superegos can be very sophisticated. A number of students I have worked with have had superegos that contributed to their internal emotional tone without sharing any direct judgments. Think of it as a tone of disapproval rather than a sharp, pointed attack. The air of disapproval can be harder to witness or recognize. It is subtle, and we are so acclimated to it that we may not notice it at first. Additionally, there can be superegos that will be flattering as well as condemning. The flattering superego is saying things like "No one could have done that better" or "You are the smartest person in the world." We can see that these positive superego judgments are just as problematic as the negative ones because they can create a tone of elevated approval, narcissistic grandiosity, in our inner landscape. This can be pleasant to experience. But it is false. Whatever is false in our self-definition and self-perception must ultimately be rejected, if not replaced.

If any superego pronouncement is false,
we must not let it land, or hold it, as a truth.

We must look objectively at the superego's pronouncements, whether positive or negative, with the lens of truth or what I call the "compass of truth." Is what the superego is saying thoroughly true? We can accept and integrate only truth, regardless of its source. If any superego pronouncement is false, we must not let it land, or hold it, as a truth.

The superego supports many other self-structures in our psyche. It keeps the good, pure, innocent one in operation by shielding it from the truth of reality. The superego contributes to our feeling young, vulnerable, and incapable when we are faced with a new, untried task. The inner dialogue is *Maybe I would try it, but I am not very strong or grown. I better stay where I am rather than risk being destroyed or harmed.* We need to learn to work with the superego as we progress on the spiritual path, or we will stay fixed in an outdated identity.

Details on working directly with the superego can be found in my chapter on "Orientation and Preparation" in *Demystifying Awakening.* As we do this work, the superego begins to lose its unchallenged, unquestioned, and complete power. This softening begins the lengthy conversion of the superego into a type of wise inner guide.

Narcissism

Narcissism is a lynchpin of our self-identity structure. We must engage narcissism to commence the work of deconstructing what is false and converting it to what is true about the sense of self. Narcissism is the excessive elevation of our abilities or highlighting of our sense of self to others. In some cases, the greater our perceived core wound, the greater our need for narcissism to aggrandize our sense of self inwardly and outwardly. Those children and adults who feel a great gulf between their sense of self and the inherent unity of the Absolute are compelled to constantly assert their competence, importance, and overall greatness. In simple terms, this is the lifelong desperation of the loss of self-esteem.

Those who received the least attuned mirroring as youngsters may experience the arising and functioning of grandiose narcissism. The grandiose narcissist is one who is compelled to constantly seek excessive attention, recognition, and validation. Every conversation must constantly return to their accomplishments and successes, as they attempt to elevate their shaky sense of self. The grandiose narcissist is trying desperately to convince themselves that they have inherent value.

When another person fails to see our unique specialness and mirror or reflect it back to us as we want to be seen, we feel the loss of the tenuous contact with the Absolute's Presence. Often when this profound loss is directly perceived through another's misattunement to our projected greatness, we land in the deep felt sense of a wound, a painful vulnerability of unspeakable hurt. This is a hurt that cannot be soothed by us or others, let alone repaired or healed in any fashion. Our fear of this core wound prevents us from directly engaging it effectively. We feel we are doomed to a life of agonizing misery and crushing, indescribable loss.

Whenever another person intentionally or inadvertently brushes up against this core egoic deficiency, we typically react with anger, rage, envy, jealousy, and unquenchable, unexpressed grief. The resulting reminder of our core wound leads to us creating and asserting an air of superiority, repeating, *My way, my view, is one-hundred-percent right.* This supports an artificial sense of entitlement and undermines our ability to deeply connect or empathize with others.

For some people directly working the core wound, particularly after *kenshō*, both the felt sense of this loss of contact with the Absolute Presence and the self's allegiance to its narcissistic self-structuring result in the creation of a shell of identity. This shell of identity is formed around our consciousness as protection for our fragile egoic structures, our core wound, and ultimately our perceived sense of self. This shell or container may be felt as metal, wood, rubber, plastic, glass, etc. We feel and, to some degree, know we are fake—inauthentic. Regularly feeling our fakeness, our phoniness, is disturbing to us, and it propels us to constantly assert the sense of self, the personality structures, ostensibly covering and intending to distract from our aching core wound.

Our narcissism only begins to resolve as we contact our true nature, the Absolute, functioning in and as our consciousness.

Our ignorance of our psychological structures restricts the deepening and amplification of realization.

Transforming Dysfunction into Authenticity: An Overview

In engaging a life of spiritual practice, including prayer and meditation, it is important to be mindful of our psychological structures, because without understanding, we become destined to act unconsciously from these structures, harming both ourselves and those around us. Our ignorance restricts the deepening and amplification of realization.

Supported by greater understanding of our psychological structures, we can more effectively work through the day-to-day experiences of our core wound's effects, a process I explore in depth in Part 1 of this book, "Revealing and Updating."

Here is an example of what that process might look like. Perhaps your core deficiency manifests in a moment of driving as you maneuver your car to be the first to merge into traffic. When we feel that we need to assert ourselves to feel seen, that is the core deficiency. On some level, you might think, *Unless I beat the other cars to the front of the line, they will confirm I am worthless—a loser, a failure.*

When in a suitable place, write in your spiritual journal about the experience of needing to be first in line. Feel into how you felt immediately before you pursued winning over everyone else. What was the felt sense of deficiency? Feel the egoic emptiness, the sense of failure, of despondent loss. Let your body assume the posture of failure—hunched shoulders, weak body, sad expression. Feel deeply the sense of failure, the invisibility at your core. You may feel, *I just don't matter* or *No one cares.*

Breathing deeply, sense where in your body you feel the somatic experience of failure, of egoic emptiness. Perhaps it is in the belly and solar plexus. Maybe it feels weak and quivering. Stay with the feeling, the bodily felt sense. Feel the boundaries of this sense of failure, of worthlessness.

As you clearly locate the sense of weakness or failure in your belly and solar plexus, slowly explore the question I will discuss later in the book: What else is here? What else can you feel in your body? You will be surprised to learn there are likely other beneficial sensations and experiences in your body just waiting to be revealed.

There have been times when I have found a deep, shameful weakness in my belly. In first contact there is a belief that this is the totality of my inner experience. Yet, in investigating what else is here, I find a place of peace. What can peace be doing here? Doesn't the peace know what a shameful failure I feel myself to be?

Feel the weakness and quivery failure in your solar plexus at the same time as you feel the peace in your heart. Let each have its own space. Do not try to change anything. Just be with both—together. Let them interact. In the fullness of time these two felt-sense experiences will begin to communicate, to interact. Change can happen through this interaction.

The peace soothes the shameful sense of failure. The sting of shame softens and becomes lighter. This begins to remedy and heal our deep belief that we are a failure, an impostor in our own life.

As we work through recognized experiences of egoic deficiency, like this one, we update our self-definition—the way we see ourselves. We may begin to see that the underlying belief that we are worthless is not fundamentally true. We may feel a sense of superficiality in our self-belief. I may hold an opinion that I am worthless, but staying with the underlying belief, I can sense and feel it is hollow, fake, a mental construction. It is not ultimately real.

Whenever we reject what is historic and false,
we introduce today's reality.

When we identify an aspect of our self-belief that is not true, we cannot maintain it. We cannot keep it close. It must be rejected and released as fake and false.

Whenever we reject what is historic and false, we introduce today's reality. Our reality is that we may not be the finest person on this planet, yet we are not the most abject failure either. Perhaps we can confirm we are okay right now.

Changing our self-belief from complete failure to a bit of a failure with occasional redeeming qualities, we begin to convert karma from negative to positive. Holding close experiences and memories where we failed, where our deficiency was confirmed, is negative karma. Seeing that that belief is not always true loosens the grip of that belief, which in turn invites positive karma, the objective truth of who we are. *Sometimes I am okay*, I feel at this point.

Whenever we begin to convert negative karma to positive karma, we begin to change also the underpinnings of who we take our self to be—our self-identity. In effect we are updating, we are rewriting, our self-identity code. This is an earth-shattering event. Our sense of self that we see as unchangeable has been modified and changed based on direct experience. This is a minor liberation from the oppression of the customary sense of self.

In Part 1 of this book, "Revealing and Updating," I walk you through the steps for working through challenging emotional states and uncovering the qualities of true nature embedded within them. In the first chapter of Part 1, "Foundational Practices," you will find instructions for keeping a daily spiritual journal and for what-else-is-here practice. For recognizing and managing discomfort and other resistances to this process of revealing and updating self-identity, I have included an innate goodness meditation with I-am-not and I-am practices, as well as off-the-cushion equanimity and compassion meditations. In "Working with Specific Challenging Emotions," the second chapter of Part I, we look beyond the surface presentations of hatred, anger, weakness and insecurity, envy and jealousy, guilt, greed and resentment, and cruelty in order to explore how these emotions distort authentic, unconditioned qualities of the Absolute. In each case, I have provided guidance for contacting and practicing with the challenging emotions and associated qualities of the Absolute, insight into accompanying resistances, questions to inspire reflection, and lessons shared from my own experiences.

Part II of the book, "Unwinding and Releasing," complements Part I by presenting practices that deconstruct concepts that support the belief in a me, allowing us to let go of the constructed identity intertwined with our mind workings. In other words, we return to zero, to nothing, each time we undertake one of these meditative practices. There are three chapters in Part II, offering *samatha* (purification-of-mind) practices, protective meditations, and *shikantaza* (silent illumination meditation), respectively. The *samatha* practices and meditations deliberately and slowly deconstruct our firm belief in the sense of self. Through identifying and uncovering the components that make up and support the sense of self, we discover that our self, the me, cannot be located anywhere in the body. The protective meditations support our deepening practice and the gradual releasing of the belief in a me. We do this through the practice of the protective meditations, which are *mettā* (love), the positive attributes of the Buddha, deep contemplation on a decaying corpse, and recollection of our own death. *Shikantaza* is a deep meditation practice that allows us to recognize inner unity, see the body boundary as a primary sense of self, and open to direct and immediate contact with the qualities and functions of the Absolute.

In each of these practices we are orienting to the truth of direct experience. We are electing to bring awareness to the felt sense of our meditative object so the focus of each meditation rests beneath the conceptual knowing.

What is the difference between conceptual and nonconceptual knowing? When we are practicing at the conceptual level (the level of thought and memory), we are regularly comparing and contrasting the object of our attention with words, experiences, understandings, and memories. For example, if I ask you to close your eyes and intuitively contact some location in your body that is "hardness," what do you contact? Initially most people would locate a bone, nails, or teeth as hardness. Then would come the definitions, memories, and stories about hardness. All these would be the conceptual understanding. It is relating a direct experience to historic concepts of understanding and deeply held beliefs in the sense of self.

When we can become meditatively concentrated enough, we can drop beneath the conceptual level of understanding and processing to that area of mind that knows without idea, judgment, thought, or memory. It is without concept. If you were to attempt to tell me about your nonconceptual contact with hardness in our example, you would have no words with which to express hardness to me. You would have to find a manner of expression that was nonconceptual and nonverbal.

It is important to practice at the nonconceptual level, particularly during an in-person retreat. When we contact and operate from nonconceptual reality, we are experiencing nature as it experiences itself. We are experiencing life directly without mental overlay or meaning. In doing so, we feel a kind of freedom, and we open to deeper and deeper intuitive knowing. Intuitive knowing allows the wisdom of the Absolute to shine through our perceptions and experiences. It is ideal to work with a realized teacher who is deeply and directly experienced in the nonconceptual approach to these practices. Practicing them without a qualified teacher can lead to a practitioner having an unwitting conceptual experience and a reinforcing of their sense of self.

Few teachers can guide students into territories they themselves have not mastered, so choose one carefully. Locate a teacher who resonates with truth in a way you can see. Ask yourself, *Will I be content if I live from a similar realization?* A teacher who has traversed the portion of the path you are on can help you identify and meet the challenges and difficulties that can, and will, arise on an authentic path of liberation. They can validate and confirm what is happening while encouraging you onward. It is advisable both to attend in-person retreats the teacher offers and to work with them one-on-one at least once a month. This deepens the relationship while inviting transmission of the Absolute energetic quality of the path where you are engaged.

To show how valuable it is to do this difficult work with a teacher, and to illustrate how different each person's journey can be, I have included some of my students' experiences—expressed in their own words—at regular intervals throughout this book. I hope that seeing current students advancing through the practices, living with greater authenticity, and fundamentally changing themselves for the better will be a deeply supportive experience for you, as it is for me.

No matter where you are on the path of Awakening, you, like all of us, may benefit from a reminder of our ultimate source and destination, Cessation—the experience of complete merging into the deep peace, profound stillness, and remarkable Absence of the source of the Absolute—and with it, the permanent dissolution of our constructed self-identity. This is the focus of the last two students' perspectives, provided toward the end of the book, and of the conclusion of *Liberating the Self*. It is helpful to keep this profound experience in our sights as we undertake our long, engaged journey.

"I knew my life was never going to be the same"

It was my first retreat. I came to the retreat center with the intention of Awakening. This was expressed in a kind of prayer, a mixture of gratitude, confidence, determination, humility, and surrender. I invited the Absolute to awaken in the location that is me.

For anyone who has not been, a retreat center is a true treasure. The land, while once disturbed, has completely been overtaken by nature. Thick moss, lichens, ferns, and trees everywhere—wild and unkempt. I was in awe. It was July, and the musical backdrop was primarily a contest between the Pacific wren, the tiniest bird you've ever seen, who always seems to be compensating for its size with an impossibly long and complex song, and the Swainson's thrush, high in the treetops above, giving an ethereal, spiral-like call which must have been stolen from some fairy kingdom.

This was an easy location to feel reverence for the Absolute. After a couple of days of innate goodness meditation, I was having a very pleasant unity experience that slowly built on Sunday and into Monday. At one point I remember walking through the forest saying to myself, *That is me, that is me, that is me*, about every living thing I passed. This included each insignificant weed along the trail. It was surprising to me then. It is surprising to me now. Where did that come from? Later it even expanded to inanimate human-made objects. The coffee can, *That is me, too.*

Tuesday morning, my concentration started feeling like a spotlight. This was after one of the guided Awakening meditations with Stephen Mugen Snyder, Sensei. While walking, I remember pausing, taking the spotlight, and doing one quick scan of my body looking for a self and not finding it. It was soon after that the innate goodness suddenly transformed into Absence (emptiness). It was as if innate goodness and Absence were made of the same material. I remembered the "Who am I?" question and laughed thinking the right question is "What am I?" Vast emptiness abided. The majority of my body boundary extended around me about three to four feet, but part of it extended much farther, like forty to fifty feet from the body's location. It felt like a psychotic break but in a good way. My name seemed like a very small and distant concept. It was not a personal accomplishment because the personality was not present. There was some fear at moments. *What does this mean to my life?* I wondered.

At one point I stood at the edge of a clearing in the forest, and I could feel the void extending out two hundred feet. There was a size but also a limitlessness to it. It was disconcerting, but then I could feel love around the edges of the void. Love being present surprised me. Mugen Sensei has described this unconditioned, universal love, but I never believed it fully until experiencing it for myself. Knowing the love was there helped calm me down a bit. I went back to my room to meditate more, but it was too much. I spent the rest of the afternoon relaxing outside and the Absence faded into Oneness.

Tuesday night I had a very unpleasant experience. I could feel movement in my hair and became convinced that I had gotten lice. Eventually I got to sleep, but when I woke up before 5 a.m., the sensations were still there. *This is hours later, it can't just be in my head*, I thought. I wrote a note to the retreat staff explaining that I knew it was very unlikely I would have picked up lice, but I was having this problem and needed help. I decided to take a shower before dropping off the note. Maybe shampoo would help. After the shower, I was sitting on the couch drinking coffee and meditating—definitely in my happy place—but the scalp sensations showed up again stronger than ever.

This just confirms it! I pinned my note to the staff board. But an hour later, I figured out it was all in my head. The concern of scalp activity was a worry resistance. I checked the staff board and slyly removed my note, quite relieved that nobody had gotten to it yet.

Once my imaginary lice problem was over with, the rest of Wednesday morning was quite pleasant. Innate goodness and unity everywhere. Incredible beauty everywhere. In a few feet of forest, I could find one thousand things to stare at, in awe that I had missed them the dozens of previous times I had walked the same paths. By Wednesday afternoon my old sense of self was returning. Still very pleasant, but I could also tell I was being thrown out of the Garden of Eden, out of heaven.

During the Wednesday night group meditation, things started getting interesting again. The scalp sensations returned, but this time they were very intense over the entire top of my head for the entire meditation period (and until I went to bed). This time it was very pleasant. I decided the experience was safe and started surrendering to it. In hindsight, I believe it was my crown chakra opening. After the sit, I went walking in the dark forest and the experience started going very deep again. Absence returned. It was seeing reality directly—very intensely spiritual. Very far gone. Ancient majesty and some fear for my safety.

On the final morning, before leaving the retreat center, I walked the trails one last time. I had the distinct feeling that Awakening was something I had done before, that I knew how to do it again, and that there was an inevitability to the next steps. (The first two were funny thoughts for someone who had been a longtime atheist.) I knew my life was never going to be the same. Also, I knew that I wanted to teach eventually. How could anyone experience this and not want to help others do the same? Awakening felt natural, like it is our birthright.

Functioning back in daily life was easier than I expected. You do not need a self to drive on the freeway or manage everyday life. Every capability I ever had was still present.

It was three weeks later before I had a moment of feeling "normal." But honestly, there is no going back. Many things faded but others were permanently different. For me the experience was really only positive. Beauty and connection were everywhere. My performance at work went up. My relationship with my wife improved. Compulsive behavior was reduced. Negative emotions, the defilements of mind, all reduced. I was the happiest I had ever been. It was not all smooth sailing. Integrating the experience was not easy, and it took time and ongoing support from Mugen Sensei. I was still flawed. I still had challenges and frustrations. Mistakes were made. But the baseline moved permanently. Only my wife really noticed the outward change. Internally, the experience of being me was not the same; it was better in every way.

As I write this, it is six months since that experience. That first experience at the retreat center feels like the first step on a never-ending path. Whether I travel an inch or a thousand miles on that path, for me, this is it.

—STUDENT I

"Recognizing something in my being that had long been searching for recognition"

My one-week retreat with Mugen Sensei in 2022 did not begin well. My flight to Zagreb, Croatia, was delayed by two hours. I stared at my watch, stressing about missing the one bus a day that would get me to the retreat location. In the end, I—barely—made it, but by the time I arrived I was exhausted from what would have been, even without the additional stress, a long day's travel.

The first unusual occurrence took place that night as Mugen Sensei was giving the welcome talk. Sitting there, listening to him discussing some quite mundane logistics, I suddenly felt my awareness sync into strong coherence and my reality distinctly blink out of and then, perhaps two seconds later, back into existence. This kind of Cessation phenomenon was familiar to me from a previous retreat, and it would occasionally occur in my daily practice, but it was extremely rare for it to happen in a kind of public situation, especially when I was in an emotionally agitated condition. It did not have much effect, however, on this agitated condition, which persisted for the rest of the evening, and I filed the experience away mentally as a kind of curiosity without giving it much further thought.

After a few good, uneventful days, I started to struggle. More distraction, more physical discomfort. During a walking meditation period outside, in the heat, I started to feel borderline sick. When I returned to the meditation hall, I used a chair rather than my cushion for the first time that week and sat there sweating lightly, distracted, suffering. With little warning or obvious cause, my attention and awareness began to synchronize. I drifted deeper and deeper until I found myself in a vivid hypnagogic vision, like a dream but with all the comprehensiveness and convincingness of waking reality. No sense of self or agency was present; I was simply the awareness out of which the vision unfolded—the screen, as it were, onto which the video was projected. The vision was as follows: I found myself standing in the small dining-room area of the retreat center, which had a type of porch where I was accustomed to removing and leaving my shoes. In the vision I was holding my shoes, which in the logic of the vision were my ego, my sense of self. I said to my shoes/ego, *Where I am going, I cannot take you with me. I will come back for you later.* And I bent down to place them on the ground. As the shoes/ego touched the floor, an indescribably powerful rush of energy, like a geyser, exploded up from the ground of the meditation hall, through the seat of my chair, up through my spine, out of the top of my head, and violently annihilated my experience of reality.

My next conscious experience was taking a huge, gulping inbreath and feeling powerful energetic currents running throughout my whole body. The original blast of energy had been so strong that I expected to find myself flat on my back on the floor; I was surprised to be upright still. I was extremely present, extremely alert, but I also had the strange intuition that something was off. This was confusing. While I knew that something significant had undoubtedly just happened, I didn't feel the way I thought I should have felt if it had truly been a substantial Awakening. I felt no joy, no ease, no sense of relief . . . I felt that my ability to attend to and be present with minute details of my experience had been supercharged, but I also felt restless, dissatisfied, and uncomfortable.

This persisted throughout the rest of the day. Although up to this point I had been content in the distraction-free environment of the retreat, I now craved distraction, felt bored, wanted something to take me out of myself. I was using a lot of effort in meditations, scrutinizing every detail of my experience, looking for a way out. I slept terribly.

The next morning Mugen Sensei guided the morning sit. At first, I was irritable, preferring silence. Mugen was guiding a Zen *shikantaza* practice, one feature of which is the intention to connect to the vastness that is always present in experience. Mugen had been using the word "vastness" in previous guided meditations as well, and I had been having some trouble connecting to this term, locating this vastness in my own experience. But this morning, he instead used the word "void."

When he said "void," I suddenly understood the limitlessness of the void that had always been present in consciousness, that is consciousness. My irritability fell away. This moment of recognition caused a great deal of agitation for what Mugen Sensei calls the "efforting part of experience" that was looking for a way out of the meditative dynamic I had been stuck in. The identification of the void produced excitement, lots of labeling, investigation, analysis— questions like *What is this?*, *What does this mean?*, and *What do I do with this?* whirled around my thinking space. This was a euphoric agitation, but it was agitation, nonetheless. I made my way into the breakfast line with my mind writhing. As I transferred oatmeal into a bowl, a new thought, from a much more settled part of experience, arose: *You don't have to work so hard. You can just let go.* And I did.

The experience becomes much more difficult to describe from this point forward. I sat with my breakfast outside, looking at the magnificent Croatian landscape, and felt that a kind of energetic barrier at the level of my heart center that had maintained the division of inside/outside had dissolved. Where I had been there was only the magnificent landscape. A wave of grief came over me for all the effort and energy I had put into constructing this barrier between what I had thought of as myself and the outside, and how unnecessary it had all been. How sad it was that I had tried so hard for so long to push the world away, with such futility.

This was followed by a massive outpouring of gratitude for Mugen Sensei and all my teachers, for the opportunities I had been granted to practice intensively, for my supportive fiancée, for my parents, for the other retreatants who helped create an ambiance in which such a thing could happen . . . eventually an undirected gratitude for everything, accompanied by an overwhelming feeling of humility, of incredible good fortune. This feeling of gratitude became steadily more intense during the next sitting period, and I began to sob copiously, blowing my nose into a paper towel from time to time, trying (and likely failing) to be discreet.

The intensity subsided at the conclusion of the sitting period, and as I walked outside before the next sit, I wondered if I was heading for a calmer, less dramatic phase of the experience. It transpired that I was not. When I sat down again—fortunately armed with extra paper towels—a sensation of deep, even primal, fear arose in my chest. This was accompanied by a different kind of vision, not so clear and vivid as the shoes/ego situation described earlier but rather more intuitive. In it I looked down on myself as a small child of perhaps three years old, lying in the fetal position with his thumb in his mouth, at the bottom of a deep hole, something like a well or a mine shaft. I intuitively understood that I was feeling the fear of this extraordinarily vulnerable young child, and at that moment came an upsurge of compassion orders of magnitude greater than anything I had known previously. I was utterly overwhelmed by the sadness I felt for this child, for the seemingly limitless quantity of fear and pain that was in him, and I sobbed through the remainder of the period even more copiously than before. When this part of experience finally subsided, I felt a powerful sense of catharsis, of wholeness, of having recognized something in my being that had been searching for recognition for a very long time.

l was utterly relieved to get to my interview with Mugen Sensei, who confirmed my intuition about what was happening and gave me a critical sense of support and safety in a moment of surprising vulnerability. Over the next days, weeks, and months, a great deal of personal material continued to come up for me, but this concludes the narrative of the core experience itself and its immediate aftermath.

—STUDENT 2

PART I

Revealing and Updating

A SPIRITUAL JOURNEY is not about achieving perfection or escaping human life. It is a constant, engaged journey of revealing and witnessing objective, universal truth while opening and gently challenging our deep-seated personal beliefs and convictions about who and what we are. In Part 1 of this book, we will learn to honestly see who we are and what lifelong conceptual convictions keep us looped into supporting and presenting a particular me to the world. In effect, we will learn how to recognize our personality beliefs, update those to more accurately reflect our true identity, and function as a wholesome wave on the ocean of the Absolute.

> *Each experience of our true self,*
> *our true nature, is enlivening.*

It is fairly common for those of us walking a spiritual path with commitment to have seconds, moments, flashes when the perception of body and mind fall or drop away. Somehow who we took ourselves to be is not here. These flashes typically last a few seconds or minutes at most. These brief experiences give us small bites of reality. We can then digest each experience, understanding that we know something new based on experience, not thought or concept. The direct experience builds trust in the path, in the teacher, and in the possibilities of realization on the horizon.

Each experience of our true self, our true nature, is enlivening. We know we are seeing our deepest truth firsthand, unmeditated, and directly. The experience is, *This is what I am. I am this.* Our trust builds toward what is presently unknown. We are willing to walk a little farther on this dimly lit path, not knowing fully where we are, who might be with us, and where we are going. This is the expression of our trust in the process of grace.

What is true nature? Each individual consciousness is always an undivided part or portion of the Absolute realm. The Absolute has two primary functions: manifest and unmanifest. The manifest is marked by the functions of pure unconditioned love, pure Presence (Beingness), and pure direct awareness (awareness without reflective capacity). The other primary function of the Absolute is the unmanifest. The unmanifest is characterized by Absence (emptiness), deep peace, and pristine stillness. The manifest often appears visually as the brightest whiteness one has ever witnessed. The unmanifest, on the other hand, typically presents visually as a rich, smooth blackness. The term "true nature" refers to the Absolute realm and its many qualities or features available in a particular consciousness. These qualities include peace, strength, support, compassion, power, joy, unconditioned love, empathetic joy, and equanimity, all emanating from the pure love, pure Presence, and pure awareness that are the manifest functioning of the Absolute. When these qualities function together, there is a sheer power, a potency, that propels the presence and love of the manifest Absolute into all reality, in all forms. The qualities of true nature from the unmanifest Absolute function as peace, stillness, and Absence.

The qualities of true nature are unconditioned, by which I mean they are not born and do not die. They have always existed and will always exist, abiding in the Absolute endlessly. They are also objective, which means that our perception and experience of the Absolute are without any personal overlay; there is no me influencing the perception and expression of the Absolute. Ironically, the Absolute is both completely intimate and nonpersonal. The Absolute does not favor any particular person or religion. All are held equally without regard for human conditioning or healthy functioning.

During our spiritual journey, it is common to encounter resistances, blocks that slow our contact with and application of the pure qualities of true nature. In the following sections we will examine many of these, so they are easier to recognize and manage. In effect, each quality of true nature is covered by layers of resistances in the form of concepts and beliefs about ourselves and how the world operates. As these resistances are vigorously questioned and challenged by the truth of direct experience, the caked-on beliefs begin to crumble, falling away to reveal the beauty and impeccably pristine functioning of true nature's qualities.

Resistances can be intertwined with our survival instincts. Making direct contact with inner reactions that conflict with our cherished self-image can feel risky. This is where we must be committed to truth. It is critical to choose being with the foundational truth of any situation over protecting or reifying our historic sense of self. This may sound daunting, but we are simply learning to feel fully whatever is in our experience, by which I mean we are neither rejecting nor clinging to anything; we can digest and release whatever is passing through. This is a function of freedom.

We can be real. We can be with the truth of each moment without preference or hierarchy.

Accepting what is actually here, in our direct perception and experience, frees us from our limited self-view. We can release the belief that we are always a good person who never has difficult emotions or strong reactions to the events of life. We can be real. We can be with the truth of each moment without preference or hierarchy.

Working with a teacher you trust will support your exploration, your journey, into the depths of your psyche to meet and question the truth of these closely held self-images and self-definitions.

CHAPTER 1

FOUNDATIONAL PRACTICES

THIS SECTION CONTAINS instructions and guidance for several supportive practices for revealing true nature and updating self-identity, as well as recognizing and managing discomfort and other resistances you may experience during this process.

Daily Spiritual Journal

I am a proponent of maintaining a spiritual journal. It is needed to record new approaches or techniques we try and any developments we see in our meditation practice, as well as times when we are in the zone—finding success taking our meditation off the cushion into our everyday life. (You can read more about this in the introduction to my book *Demystifying Awakening*.) We can also use a journal as a space for reflections when we are struggling or advancing with our meditation or life. This is important information to share with your trusted personal teacher, as it allows them to see patterns of reactivity and response and offer assistance.

A spiritual journal is a good repository for memories that arise out of the stillness of meditation, too. Often these memories arise because we are in a place to more fully understand the choices we, or others, made. These remembered memories may contain a key of sorts for understanding the origin of our core wound, which is created when we are toddlers and is the foundation for whatever personality structuring we have constructed to best navigate our birth family and early life. Our early life choices condition the filters with which we view ourselves and the world around us, including our close familial and personal relationships.

Maintaining a spiritual journal and working continually with a teacher you deeply trust can offer an opportunity to authentically rewrite your story of who you are and help you begin to see new, improved choice points in your everyday life.

Daily Spiritual Journaling

In a quiet moment of your day, turn to your journal. Write down any thoughts or feelings that arise as you do the following:

1 Reflect upon the day. Notice any memories that feel off or unsettled.
2 Examine one of these memories. Establish what exactly in that memory is unsettling to you. Was it an assumption you made, your choice of language, your actions, or some other unsettling aspect of the exchange or engagement?
3 Delve into your history with that behavior or opinion. What is the earliest memory you have of acting or reacting in a similar circumstance? When did this thought or behavioral pattern start? Why did it start?
4 When you feel you have probed the unsettling event as thoroughly as is possible, replay the scene from that day, changing your behavior, words, or actions. Sitting here, with the benefit of hindsight, how would you wish to respond to that same situation again?
5 How does the new response feel?

6   Set an intention to act in the new, congruent
    manner when you find yourself in a similar
    interpersonal dynamic with another.

This practice affords you the opportunity to
change your behavior and act more congruently
with your inner Awakening. Observing, identifying,
and modifying our behavior is the most reliable and
repeatable method to institute behavioral change.

What Else Is Here?

This is an important practice to include in your meditation toolkit. When we are struggling with a difficult memory or experience, it is helpful to locate its presence in our body. Where exactly is it somatically? We presume it occupies the entire body and mind. One learning from this practice is that when strong emotions or reactions, like hatred or anger, are present, they rarely fill our entire inner awareness. We can see that they are smaller than we first thought. This practice is very helpful for quantifying a challenging thought-emotion and noticing it is not overwhelming your body or consciousness. It is, in reality, quite manageable to be with.

When you have a clear picture or felt sense of where the emotion is located in your body, ask yourself, *What else is here?* This opening allows us to find other qualities or attributes within. You may be quite surprised to locate peace or joy or another seemingly contrasting feeling in your body. Typically, it is a quality that will be beneficial. Opening to both lets the perceived qualities communicate and interact directly. This often results in the neutralization of the difficult emotion or experience.

What-Else-Is-Here Practice

The following are the approximate steps I use for my own practice and with students. You may use your spiritual journal (see "Daily Spiritual Journaling") to record your responses and reflections if you choose.

1 Locate a clear somatic (bodily felt) sense of where the challenging emotion is abiding presently.
2 See what else is here, somatically, in addition to the difficult emotion being investigated.
3 Trace this emotion back to an early memory of it.
4 Replay that early memory as exactly as it occurred as is possible.
5 Investigate how that memory and interaction established your relationship and reaction to the difficult emotion.
6 Replay the early memory being you as you are today.
7 Ask yourself, *How would I act or respond differently today than I did when I was quite young?*
8 When you feel you have fully gleaned all you can from the original and updated memory, look for a later memory involving this same emotion. Try

to find memories that appear or feel to have a kind of frame of light around them. (I have found in my own practice the highlighted memories are usually pivotal in some manner, making them the most advantageous to work with.)

9 Repeat steps 4 through 8.

10 Continue in this manner until you have worked with each of the memories of the emotion or feeling you are exploring.

11 Stay with the felt sense of the emotion without trying to change or modify any aspect of it. Just be . . .

12 Typically, that felt sense of the emotion will open, in its own way, to the underlying, unconditioned quality of the Absolute, residing in your consciousness as your true nature. Allow the unconditioned quality of true nature to meet, open, and reside fully in your body and consciousness.

Innate Goodness

Usually, in our lives we receive mirroring of our goodness when we do something a parent, caregiver, or teacher praises. It is when we behave the way they wish that we feel seen and most importantly valued and cherished. Yet receiving this attention is being seen and valued for what we do rather than for who we are. This recognition lands as hollow, insignificant, and meaningless. This leads us to equate our goodness with what we do rather than with our innate Beingness. Concurrently, we devalue our Beingness.

Innate goodness is not dependent on any behavior or way of performing. It is an unconditioned heart-love radiance from the Presence of your Beingness. Innate goodness is a quality of your deeper or true nature, the happy, childlike joy we can witness in early pictures of ourselves or others. In contacting your innate goodness, you will feel more at ease and more positive about yourself, and you will have greater capacity to be with *dukkha* (unsatisfactoriness) in your life.

Innate goodness is a heart meditation practice that is revolutionary because we are opening to an unconditioned quality of love from our deeper or true nature, inviting it into our awareness, and gently challenging the ongoing inner, personality-driven narration defining our world. One of the benefits of innate goodness meditation is its ability to counteract both our negative self-talk and our self-judgments. I do not mean to say self-talk and self-judgments are eliminated entirely. Instead, their importance in our belief system is lessened when we practice innate goodness meditation. I will walk through the foundational meditation, then teach two new practices, "I am not" and "I am," for before and during meditation. (For more teachings related to innate goodness practice, including resistances and my own experience with it, see "Innate Goodness Meditation" in Chapter 4.)

Innate Goodness
Meditation Practice

- Close your eyes. Seat yourself in a comfortable position. Place your hands in your lap or high on your thighs. Take a few deep, settling breaths, inhaling and exhaling as thoroughly as possible.
- Feel your feet on the ground while noticing the support of the floor in the building you are in. If you can, feel Mother Earth beneath holding, supporting, and offering each of us nourishment in this very moment. This very breath is a gift of life from our Mother Earth.
- For the visual meditator: Picture yourself—or another being, nature itself, or an idealized figure such as Jesus, Buddha, or the Dalai Lama—in your mind's eye.
- For the felt-sense meditator: Remember a time when you were near a baby, a young child, an idealized spiritual figure, or a sweet-natured animal, perhaps a pet. How did it feel energetically to be in contact with them?
- In both cases, recall the sweet goodness the being radiates. Recall how they do not need to do anything to radiate innate goodness; their presence

alone has a goodness in it. That's the goodness
we are touching into in this meditation.

— Maintain your awareness in your heart region.
You may feel a sensation of a flow, a sense of
goodness, okayness, warmth, or freshness in the
heart area when innate goodness is present. You
will be able to confirm it is innate goodness by
its objective and universal feel as it is a quality
of your true nature. Whatever is emanating
from true nature in our consciousness is arising from the Absolute. It is unconditioned,
meaning it is not born and does not die. It feels
self-generative since there is no start or finish to
that heart quality. By contrast, when we create
a thought-emotion, there is a quality of me in
it. It is like the emotion has my scent or another
identifying marker embedded within it.

— Be with the picture, in your mind's eye or with
the felt sense of innate goodness, for ten minutes
or more without serious interruption. When the
picture or felt sense of innate goodness is readily
apparent, try lessening or dropping the visual or
felt-sense object of the other being to generate
direct contact with innate goodness.

— Rest your awareness directly in, and with, innate
goodness. In effect, let your awareness merge
into innate goodness.

I-Am-Not Practice

The I-am-not practice disidentifies with the functions of being human. Orienting to what we are not helps us open to and experience what we are— our unconditioned true nature.

In your meditation posture, after some deep full-belly breaths, repeat the following out loud or silently:

1   "I am not this appearance."
2   "I am not this body."
3   "I am not these thoughts."
4   "I am not this life history."
5   "I am not these behaviors."
6   "I am not these emotions."
7   "I am not these memories."
8   "I am not these identities."
9   "I am not anything."

This practice can be done before the innate goodness meditation to help loosen the "markers of me." It can also be used during meditation. For example, if you are meditating and notice a distracting memory arising, you can say silently, *I am not these memories*. This can help the memory soften and fade before you get too engaged with it.

I-Am Practice

Another helpful related practice is "I am." When we
are present in the vast, unending inner spaciousness
or deeply resting in innate goodness, we can turn
to the I-am practice. The I-am practice orients our
awareness specifically toward the Presence function
of the Absolute.

— Softly and silently say, *I*, making certain you treat
  it very lightly.
— Then focus awareness on the "am." The am is
  a portal to deepen contact with the Presence
  function of the Absolute. Silently repeat, *Am, am,
  am*. Doing so in your meditation, when deeply
  resting within, draws awareness more fully
  into Presence.

NOTE: If you are well seated in your meditation, you
may not need to use the I portion of the practice.
The I can cause us to orient toward the customary
sense of self and its structures. In effect, it can land
us more fully in the me that we are trying to soften,
purify, and release. If you do not need the I as part of
the practice, exclusively focus on am.

Off the Cushion

I have written extensively on the ancient Buddhist heart practices, called the *brahmavihāras* or "divine abodes," in my book *Buddha's Heart*. Nonetheless, there are two *brahmavihāras* that have special relevance for lessening compulsive obedience to our sense of self and for opening the flower of Awakening: *upekkhā* (equanimity) and *karuṇā* (compassion). I am going to present the off-the-cushion practice application of these two *brahmavihāras*.

On-the-cushion meditation is extremely important. We need to learn to be quiet and listen to the source—the Absolute. The peace and stillness of the Absolute reveals all. This work is complemented by off-the-cushion meditation, which we engage in when we are walking around and functioning in our life. The mature spiritual path involves learning to develop continuity, and that continuity between on-the-cushion and off-the-cushion meditation is really what deepens our practice.

Equanimity Meditation

Upekkhā is the Pali name for equanimity. Equanimity is a deep acceptance of whatever is occurring in this very moment. Many of our struggles and challenges in everyday life come from our resistance(s) to what is naturally unfolding. We have specific ideas about how life should be happening. When life does not meet our expectations, we feel let down, sad, and even depressed.

Cultivating the ability to more deeply accept what is actually happening in any given moment reduces our resistance to the moment and hence diminishes much of our anguish. Simply put, we are happier. Deep acceptance means not resisting, in any manner, our conflicting ideas or preferences. Equanimity feels balanced, perfect (even if imperfect), smooth, deeply accepting. Equanimity does not want anything to change regardless of its impact or effect. (For a more detailed exploration of equanimity, see "Greed and Resentment: A Distortion of Equanimity [*Upekkhā*]" in Chapter 2.)

Equanimity
Meditation Practice

— Imagine that you have a magical remote control in your hand. You can rewind, fast-forward, or stop this very moment. When you desire to reach for this remote and alter the flow of time, that is a tip-off that you are not fully accepting the truth of this moment. Something about the present moment has you trying to change what is right here. When you feel that urge to recoil from this moment, to employ your time remote control, you are not accepting the truth of this moment.

— Silently repeat, *Acceptance, acceptance*, with an intention to relax into this very moment.

— Feel the fullness of the moment.

— See if you can locate the part of you that has such a strong reaction to what is naturally occurring in your experience.

— If you see a personality pattern or an egoic deficiency (an inner place of discomfort), note this in your spiritual journal to work on individually or with your teacher at a later date.

In engaging "acceptance, acceptance" when meeting an unwelcome moment, we relax into this moment. We soften our resistance to what is here so that we can more fully meet what is happening and witness our reactivity to this moment. In effect, we will suffer less by accepting more and resisting less.

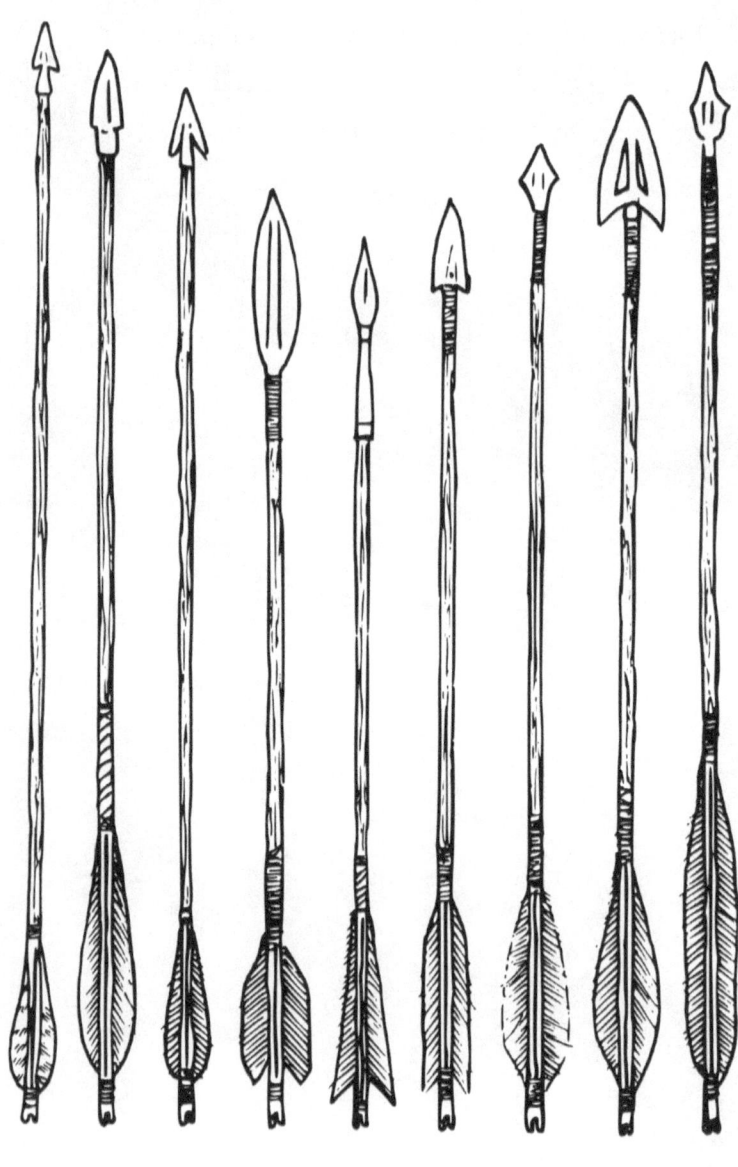

Compassion Meditation

In his teaching, the Buddha used concepts called "the first arrow" and "the second arrow." The first arrow is pain or initial discomfort. The second arrow is the story about or resistance to the first arrow. A few examples of a second arrow are *I do not deserve this, This always happens to me,* and *Why me?* You can see the obvious discomfort and pain of the second arrow.

When we experience the first arrow, we want to employ *upekkhā*, discussed previously, to offer "acceptance, acceptance." This lets us land more fully right here, right now. Once we more readily accept this moment, we turn to the challenge of the second arrow. With compassion of the Absolute, we learn to stay with neutral or unpleasant events. Compassion (*karuṇā*) is the tenderhearted, loving support of the Absolute. It affords us the potential to be present to, to witness, to hold the difficulties (the *dukkha*) of human existence.

With compassion, we turn toward unpleasantness and soften to its contact. Doing so offers us opportunities to grow as well as to support others with tender loving care through their life challenges. By reducing our fear reaction to perceived potential harmful events, we learn to understand and cultivate more accepting neutrality toward life. We become less afraid of our own life and the eventual loss of it. (For a more detailed exploration of compassion, see "Cruelty: A Distortion of Compassion [*Karuṇā*]" in Chapter 2.)

Compassion Meditation Practice

- Turning as fully as is possible toward the *dukkha*, feel the fullness of your discomfort. Notice where exactly in your body you feel the suffering or pain. (It would be common when first experiencing your pain to be convinced it is in your entire body and mind. In effect, all of you is pain. *That is how large and overwhelming the pain is,* you might think or say. The reality is that most of the pain and suffering we experience is located in a part of our body, not the whole body. I have witnessed this with hundreds, if not thousands, of students over the years I have been teaching. By more fully feeling our pain, we get in direct contact with the pain itself, and we often will find that it is more manageable immediately.)
- In a statement, report your emotional suffering. This can be "I am sad," "This hurts," or even "It is hopeless." All of these convey suffering, pointing primarily to the second arrow of judgment.
- Feel the underlying feeling referred to in the statement. Try to locate it. Where exactly does this hurt? Let us imagine you report that your heart hurts. Try to be more specific. Where in

your heart does it hurt? Where in your heart does it not hurt? Right away we see it is not the totality of your heart that is feeling sad.

- Be close to this feeling in its source. By doing so, you relax the judgment or second arrow and feel the initial hurt directly. Typically, you will feel less pain than you did initially.

- Next, feel this feeling everywhere else in your body, except in the previous location. We want to directly engage the exact components of our perceived suffering. Knowing what and where we are suffering opens us more fully to the tender, warmhearted compassion of the Absolute.

- Now you can investigate the pain or discomfort a little more directly. For example, ask yourself, *What is the sadness? Why is it here? What memory is the sadness stimulating?* This investigation can lead to learning more about our history with the feeling and how it is used as a reaction to a certain type of uncomfortable experience in our life.

What you are witnessing here is the digestion of older patterns of reactivity and a slight transformation of the sense of self to a more accurate, up-to-date self-definition.

CHAPTER 2

WORKING WITH SPECIFIC CHALLENGING EMOTIONS

A COMMON MISUNDERSTANDING about deep Buddhist practice is that we orient exclusively to transcendent, blissful, joyful experiences, engaging in what would amount to a pattern of spiritual bypass whenever we are confronted with difficult or unpleasant emotional states. But happiness and contentedness are actually only occasional by-products of a deep, sustained spiritual practice. They are not the goals.

We must have a rigorous devotion to truth,
in any form.

The compass for journeying deep into the Absolute is the compass of truth. We must have a rigorous devotion to truth, in any form. To update our self-identity, we each need to learn how to recognize and open to difficult, uncomfortable emotions or patterns of personality. Our identity is constructed, in part, out of both our active likes, dislikes, and preferences, and our historic reactions to negative emotions and behaviors. This means that the rejection or repression of historic emotions shapes our sense of self. For example, if we have difficulty responding to and expressing anger in a healthy, mature manner when life events trigger our anger, we may bury the emotion and its causation deep in our subconscious and feel overwhelmed instead. Although the anger is hidden from our view, it is nonetheless leaking and spilling into our consciousness.

There are several benefits to working directly with challenging emotional responses. First, by revealing our history and familial response pattern, we lessen and release energy and beliefs about these emotions. This released energy supplements the energy we bring to our meditation and spiritual practices. Second, our sense of self is altered by the maturation of our relationship to difficult emotional responses. If I take myself to be someone who cannot naturally express hatred, for example, that is part of my self-definition. As my functional relationship to hatred changes and early memories are witnessed and released, that part of my self-definition changes, too. Literally, I become a different person through this important work. Our sense of self not only updates to more accurately reflect who and what we are today but also opens us to deepening contact with the Absolute, as we release outdated patterns of personality.

In the following sections, I will demonstrate how to approach and engage challenging emotions and outdated personality patterns. With deepening meditation practice, we meet more resistances as we delve into our relationship and history with challenging emotions. These emotions, personality patterns, and resistances, too, need to be more fully understood as we release them in favor of more congruent, up-to-date behaviors and opinions, so we will be exploring common resistances as well.

Hatred: A Distortion of Authentic Peace and Power

In general, Buddhists are challenged by the appearance of hatred in their consciousness. Buddhists typically see themselves as warm, heart-based people who love all and care for the world around them. They may deny the experience of hatred, which I define as a longing for the offending person or object to be completely vanquished, vaporized out of existence, removed from our life.

Yet each person, unless they are deeply realized as true nature, as the Absolute, has hatred reactions to life events. There is more going on beneath the surface of our consciousness than we can possibly perceive or admit to ourselves. When we acknowledge the arising of hatred, we can then engage it and perceive that it is an emotional response to unwelcome events. As we continue on this journey, we can trace back the thought-emotion to its source in the Absolute. Making this connection opens us to contact the quality or function of the Absolute in lieu of turning to the thought-emotion of hatred in response to life events.

Hatred has two presentations. The first is the blindly destructive expression of hatred. Someone or something has upset me to such a deep degree that I want them ripped into pieces and vaporized. There is a lot of deliberate activity and doing in the inner experience of this expression of hatred. The second presentation of hatred is icy cold—the assassin. This is that numbingly cold inner sense that if we could remorselessly vaporize another person or object out of existence with our eyes, our intention, we would.

Practicing with Hatred

It is common for students to struggle briefly with contacting their own hatred. Yet opening to its full impact in our inner experience allows us to be more authentic while freeing us temporarily from the limiting self-definition of always being a good person who does not harbor negative feelings or reactions.

Within a short time, students can welcome hatred and other unpopular reactions. They can each expand their self-view to see they sometimes feel hatred as a thought-emotional reaction.

I generally suggest students use a throw pillow, hand towel, or other object to twist or physically manipulate in order to feel and express the hatred deeply. It is helpful to vocalize hatred, too. Saying "I hate you" allows us to specifically address the triggering event(s) and tie it to the physical act of wringing a kitchen towel.

I have also encouraged students to use a child's plastic baseball bat to strike a couch or bed and fully feel the hatred. Let hatred empower you while your body, your limbs, your muscles express the hatred. Say whatever words arise with the feeling of hatred. Let the hatred out in a safe, private space.

> *Releasing pent-up emotions like hatred or anger also releases the energy being employed to repress the anger or hatred. This is potent energy that is needed for the journey home to the Absolute.*

After one or more intense episodes of releasing hatred, the historic repressed hatred can move through our system rather than accumulating there. Then, as hatred arises, we can recognize it, privately feel it as fully as possible, and, in feeling it, fully let it go.

Releasing pent-up emotions like hatred or anger also releases the energy being employed to repress the anger or hatred. This is potent energy that is needed for the journey home to the Absolute.

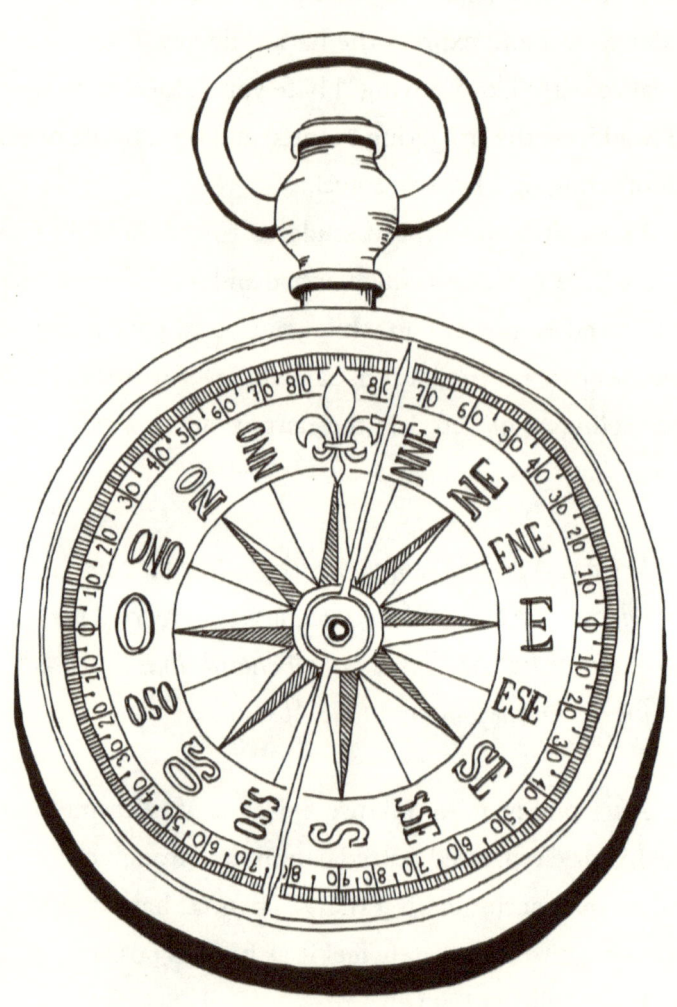

Hatred Exercise

Take a few moments to answer the following
questions in your journal:

1 What is your lifetime history and experience
   with hatred?
2 In what circumstances does hatred arise?
3 How is hatred helpful to you in your present life?

Hatred to Authentic Peace and Power

Interestingly, hatred is a distortion of two things: the deep, utter peace of the Absolute and the pure unconditioned power of the Absolute.

This is a peace that soothes the deepest contractions of hurt and pain people carry.

Conceptual peace is peace in opposition to a perceived conflict. We are focusing on authentic peace, which is smooth, expansive, spacious, and contentedly settled. There is no agitation. When I use the word "authentic," I mean to describe something that originates directly in the Absolute. Peace is a chief component of the unmanifest Absolute, along with stillness and Absence, what traditional Theravada Buddhism refers to as emptiness. This is a peace that soothes the deepest contractions of hurt and pain people carry. Peace allows us to relax our tight self-identity definition to abide more fully in not knowing who we are exactly—a state that I call "absence of self."

Authentic power is a natural expression of peace. We employ hatred as a substitute for authentic power. When we feel powerless and weak, to avoid identifying with these feelings, we turn to expressing hatred as a substitute.

When we release deep-seated historic hatred—while learning to open our self-definition to recognize and accept hatred as a possible life reaction—it loses much of its power to shame and torment us with the guilt of being a hateful person. We simply become an authentic human who has hate responses to situations where authentic, unconditioned power is not yet activated. Resting in authentic power allows us to be grounded in Presence, relaxed, and open to the mystery of the Absolute. We feel the capacity to meet any challenge or difficulty with life directly, without mediation or dilution.

Common Resistances to Authentic Peace

Resistances are the beliefs, opinions, and judgments that maintain our identification with our own suffering. Common resistances to peace include compulsion to control the life around us, identification with activity, and anxiety about surrender. Let us consider each in more detail.

- Compulsion to control life: This is an early-life personality driver. When our early-life caregivers fail to be perfectly attuned to our needs (as all caregivers end up doing), we see that our success, our happiness, our life itself is wholly dependent upon our efforts. In effect, we conclude that if we relax our effort in life, we will lose out on getting what is essentially needed.
- Identification with activity: This is expressing the belief, the conviction, that doing is the sole action or function that keeps us alive, healthy, and successful.

It is not just that we feel compelled to engage in doing to be successful. We view activity, the doingness of life, as being inseparable from who we are and our livelihood itself. For many people, this shows up in their work. Rather than explaining our work as "This is what I do," we describe ourselves as the role itself. In this way we identify with our doing as our identity.

— Anxiety about surrender: Again, control is the drug of personality structuring. We believe that if we can completely control life, we will not only survive but thrive. In the world, we constantly see examples of people who are successful. Their success usually appears tied directly to their personal effort, their drive. As a result, we may fear the consequences of surrendering control over some aspects of our life.

As we fully engage the spiritual path, we begin to learn the role and function of what I call in my teaching "proactive effort." This is our affirmative doingness. We use proactive effort at times when we must initiate action or behavior—for example, when we start a new meditation practice. When our proactive effort starts to work, we want to shift to "receptive effort," appropriate and timely minimizing or surrendering of personal effort. Simply put, receptive effort is allowing. If our timing is on point, we will feel an effortless deepening of the meditation. This is a sign that the timing and the amount of surrender is appropriate.

Resistances-to-Peace Exercise

Take a few moments to answer the following questions in your journal:

1 What is your lifetime history and experience with these resistances?
2 In what circumstances do these resistances arise?
3 How are these resistances helpful to you in your present life?

My Experience with Hatred and Authentic Peace and Power

In my birth family I perceived that anger was an unwelcome expression. I recall being punished when I displayed anger. My strategy was then to resort to the icy-cold hatred of the assassin. I would hold my cold, hard gaze upon the person or object whose very existence offended me. If, by chance, the other were vaporized out of existence by my icy stare, that would have been quite acceptable to me at that young age.

I have told some of my students a story of working with anger and hatred with one of my teachers many years ago. I was afraid of my own anger and hatred. Because anger was suppressed in my family, I held the opinion that my anger was extremely potent and would, in fact, harm others if revealed or expressed.

There happened to be a fly buzzing around the room we were in for my one-on-one session with my teacher. As the fly landed on the closed window near me, my teacher suggested I turn my deadly, angry hate-filled gaze to the fly. "Kill the fly," I was told. I was very resistant to this suggestion. I knew that should I turn this raw anger toward the fly, I would literally vaporize it out of existence.

As a Buddhist, I had taken, and received, the Buddhist One-Mind Precepts. The first of the Ten Precepts is to cultivate preciousness (see Appendix). Here I was planning to intentionally kill another being. My inner critic was working

overtime to condemn me as a bad Buddhist for consider-
ing killing a fly. Yet, a few minutes later, I was leveling my
all-powerful killing gaze at this little fly who seemed to be
napping on the warm window ledge at the time. As you can
guess, nothing happened. The fly continued to nap while I
leveled every bit of my killing anger-hatred at the fly. This
was a very powerful moment for me. It afforded me a shift
in my self-belief. I had to challenge the belief in the killing
power of my angry hate. Using the compass of truth, I had to
acknowledge my anger and hate were not too much. It was
not a risk to me or others if I simply felt the anger or hatred
when it was present.

*It was not a risk to me or others if I simply felt the
anger or hatred when it was present.*

As we become more familiar with our pattern of hatred,
it will arise in awareness rather than under the surface of
awareness. In other words, it does not function outside of
our awareness, hidden and invisible. As we work with our
patterns of hatred, we can eventually move awareness to the
moment before hatred arises as a reaction to the feelings of
powerlessness or profound weakness. Learning to be with
feelings of powerlessness will, ironically, open us to the
quality and Absolute function of peace.

In all candor, I rarely experienced peace until the first
kenshō experience. Until my inner grip on my personality

functioning was dislodged, I could not let go or open with abandon to the profound peace of the Absolute. I now often rest in peace and contentment. I find peace to be the deeply settled function of the Absolute. Conceptual peace contrasts with conflict or fighting. Authentic peace feels energetically smooth and deeply accepting. Whenever peace arises in consciousness, I find a relaxation commences. I want to unwind inner contractions or held reactions. Simply put, I let go.

Recently there was a challenging family dynamic—disagreements and friction relating to a family member's health issues and treatment choices. As there was significant emotion, mental and conceptual positions quickly became entrenched. I stepped away to sit quietly. I found that as soon as I sat with an intent to listen rather than assert my opinions, all mentalizing quieted. Awareness drifted into my heart area and into the *hara* in the belly. (The *hara* is about two fingerbreadths below the navel and about two to three fingerbreadths beneath the surface of the skin.) Simply by shifting awareness away from the head and its concepts, I felt deeply settled. In the space of ease that accompanied the settledness, I discovered a growing acceptance. I was beginning to accept the situation exactly as it was. This is an expression of equanimity (*upekkhā*), a heart practice I teach. Further, the deep, contented peace began increasing in my inner experience and perception. I could continue to let go of opinions and concepts. In this peace, I gravitated into an unknowing place. Resting in deep peace with a not-knowing mind, I was able to more fully meet the family dynamic. I had greater resources at my disposal.

Experiencing peace regularly, in meditation and daily life, opens us to a smoothness, a capacity to deeply accept and engage with whatever is happening.

Anger: A Distortion of Authentic Strength

Like hatred, anger is a reaction, an emotion, that many Buddhists discount or minimize. Because Buddhism is so focused on warmhearted acceptance, there is a cultural idealization that we do not have anger. Let me dispel that belief. Everyone has anger reactions to some life events. Typically, the experience of being minimized, ignored, or rejected triggers feelings of fear, anxiety, and hurt. In an effort to not feel fear, anxiety, or hurt, we try to exhibit strength. We want to use strength to energetically overpower the offending party and stop our hurt.

Since we are being psychologically triggered, we are not typically in contact with our true nature and its qualities such as unconditioned strength, so we turn toward the next option—anger. We lash out at the other with anger in an attempt to assert our natural, authentic strength, to demonstrate we are not hurt or fearful, and to assert some control of this situation.

Anger is not the same as strength. Anger is our substitution for unconditioned, authentic strength. When we are deeply landed and resting in our true nature, which is the Absolute in an individual consciousness, we operate less from the personality and its deficits.

> *Perfection is not avoiding all negative experiences and states of mind but rather accepting whatever is truly here in this moment, resting on this breath.*

Practicing with Anger

Deep acceptance is our goal when we work with challenging inner reactions and reactivity centers. We must accept what is here in order to fully be present. We must acknowledge that we experience anger sometimes. Perfection is not avoiding all negative experiences and states of mind but rather accepting whatever is truly here in this moment, resting on this breath.

When a situation arises in which you feel hurt or minimized, notice your inner reaction. There may be a sense of pain, anxiety, or freezing—being unable to decide what action to take. Feeling the pain, anxiety, and freezing can stimulate our fear and trigger our survival instinct. *I might be hurt if I remain frozen and uncertain*, we often say to ourselves. To crack what feels frozen, we may well lash out in anger as a strength substitute.

Lashing out in anger is intended to not only stop the source of our pain but also to demonstrate we are not weak. Anger gives us the illusion we are in control of our life. We feel that anger communicates a boundary that is not to be crossed by others.

To practice with anger, we start by opening to the surface appearance of anger when it arises. As a reminder, you do not need to express or show the anger to anyone. However, it is vital that you allow yourself to internally feel the fullness of your anger.

Ask yourself, *What does my anger feel like? Where in my body is the anger?*

When you locate where in your body the anger is present, you will likely be surprised by all the places in your body where anger is not. By being clear on where anger is, we realize it is not everywhere in either our perception or direct experience. The fact that anger is contained to a geographic area in our body suggests it is not necessarily overwhelming. If the anger was everywhere, it might, in fact, be overwhelming.

Anger Exercise

Take a few moments to answer the following
questions in your journal:

1 What is your lifetime history and experience
   with anger?
2 In what circumstances does anger arise?
3 How is anger helpful to you in your present life?

Anger to Authentic Strength

Customarily, whenever we assert strength, we have mentally decided that strength is needed in a particular situation or dynamic. We recall other times when we asserted strength and arrive at an idea about or expression of that strength. This is conceptual strength. It is an expression of our history and thoughts about strength.

Authentic strength arises nonconceptually. It is not generated by our history or thoughts. It is objective, not personal or vindictive. It never needs to assert or prove anything. Authentic strength is a force of nature.

Here is an example. I was in a group activity not long ago. One person was taking pictures of another who had just arisen from a night's sleep. The pictures were of a disheveled, sleepy person. The person taking the photos was then sending them to mutual acquaintances, giggling the whole time.

In sitting quietly, without any reactivity, I could feel the power imbalance and the quality of bullying unfolding. Instead of feeling and expressing anger, I felt an arising of clarity and transparent strength. When the bully raised their phone to take another unflattering picture, I blocked their shot, saying, "The bullying stops." The person wielding the camera looked flustered and embarrassed. I suspect they did not equate their actions with bullying. Rather, they were attracted to humor at another's expense.

Later the person who was sleep disheveled approached me and thanked me for standing up for them. In the moment I asserted authentic strength, they saw deeply the long history of being bullied by the other. To this day that same person stands up for themself in the face of ongoing bullying. That was a wonderful but unexpected benefit of the expression of authentic strength.

Authentic strength is a resting strength that supports and guides us in decisions and action.

Authentic strength allows us to engage in difficult situations or conversations without feeling inner instability and weakness. It is a resting strength that supports and guides us in decisions and actions. Authentic strength—that is, the strength of the Absolute—supports our confidence and minimizes paralyzing indecision. We are clear on the situation and on our engagement or response to the situation at hand. We do not need to assert authentic strength to prove its existence, nor do we need to brag about it or exaggerate its presence in our consciousness. The inner confidence of authentic strength allows us to rest content in the knowledge we can, and will, take decisive action.

Common Resistances to Authentic Strength

Common resistances to authentic strength include identification with weakness, helplessness, or being small; rejection of strength as being too aggressive; and fear of failure to assert strength.

— Identification with weakness, helplessness, or being small: We can find a lot of controlling, personal power in holding ourselves to be weak, helpless, or small, because many others in our societies, including spiritual practitioners, are trained and conditioned to offer compassion and support to those who seem less capable. But this is a faux strength that can be used to justify unskillful, unwholesome behavior. Should the drive for Awakening be sufficiently strong, the person who identifies as weak and helpless will try stretching outside their comfort zone to find their authentic, independent strength.

— Rejection of strength as being too aggressive: Some children witness caregivers with forceful personalities asserting their personal strength to get what they want or to bend others to conform or comply with their wishes. These children may feel overwhelmed meeting these powerful personalities, and that reaction can shift into fear as well as an intention to never be like these overbearing personalities.

— Fear of failure to assert strength: Other children in this situation may try to follow in their powerful caregiver's footsteps. But often when the child tries to assert themself in a powerful personality style, it does not go well. If others question or challenge the child's actions, the child collapses internally. They conclude they do not possess sufficient inner strength. The natural question asked is *Why should I try to assert myself or my wishes when I will only miserably fail?*

Resistances-to-Strength Exercise

Take a few moments to answer the following questions in your journal:

1 What is your lifetime history and experience with these resistances?
2 In what circumstances do these resistances arise?
3 How are these resistances helpful to you in your present life?

My Experience with Anger and Authentic Strength

At a young age, I observed family members who had terrible tempers. If they lost their temper, they would often be violent. I was often scared by their displays of anger. For me that pushed anger into a category where it was unwanted, rejected, and potentially dangerous. These were good reasons to suppress my anger as much as possible.

As I got older, this conviction that anger was an unacceptable emotion was supported by my idealization of deeply spiritual people, whom I viewed as being anger-free. I saw many senior practitioners and teachers who never seemed to get angry. They often appeared poised and content. I concluded that these folks never experienced the anger that mere mortals like me struggled with. My conclusion was reinforced by my self-identity as someone who was too weak or small to express anger without being overwhelmed and dominated by those who were stronger, which was virtually everyone.

I also had the perception that you were a brute if you gave in to your anger. I judged others harshly whenever they expressed anger, believing they were not sufficiently spiritual or even a good human if they gave in to anger impulses.

The problem with these outdated viewpoints was that they made the energy of aliveness contained in authentic strength rarely available to me. There were certainly times in my life when clear, direct, immediate action arising from authentic strength was absolutely needed. Closing off our awareness to emotional areas involving anger or hatred robs us of the natural potency and energy of these emotions. Potency and energy are needed to meet the challenges of human life. Yet we hinder ourselves when we suppress and disregard our humanity and human emotions.

> *Potency and energy are needed to meet the challenges of human life. Yet we hinder ourselves when we suppress and disregard our humanity and human emotions.*

Over time I began to see that my spiritual journey and practice needed the energy being used to hold anger at bay. The energy was needed to develop and maintain contact with realization or Awakening of the Absolute.

I worked with several teachers initially to try to locate my anger. I started by recognizing the anger when it was present. I found I was able to contact hatred rather deeply and with little restraint or suppression, but contacting anger was more difficult. My life experience to date had been that hatred was easier and safer to permit than anger. Often anger has an expression in an interpersonal dynamic. Hatred does not need outer expression in the same way. Once I was able to locate and contact the anger, I had to have very controlled circumstances to express it in small bites. I had convinced myself that suppressing my anger was the safest course. I felt

I was doing a community service by suppressing my anger. As we learn to acknowledge and accept our anger responses, we can begin not only to fully feel the anger, without necessitating outward expression, but also to realize that it is the perception of our weakness that triggers the anger as a faux strength. When we can contact the experience of weakness preceding the arising of anger, we can begin to gravitate toward the Absolute and its natural quality of strength.

One sign of the presence of authentic strength is a feeling of comfort and inner confidence. It is a strength that does not need to be exhibited or proven to anyone. We experience it as a settled confidence in our belly, called the *hara* in the Zen tradition. Resting in our authentic strength in the *hara* allows us to have a grounding, a clarity, and to be more fully present in each moment of life, regardless of the content of that moment.

I recall an interpersonal engagement I had shortly after authentic strength opened and landed in my consciousness. I had a meeting with someone who exhibited many of my early-life caregivers' traits, which I found misattuned. I was begrudgingly meeting this challenging person. When we met, the other person behaved and spoke in the manner I usually found triggering. I waited for the urge to respond defensively. Instead, I watched their behavior and speech pass right through me without landing. I had the stability and confidence of authentic strength to not be triggered by historic material or behaviors.

Weakness and Insecurity:
A Distortion of Unconditioned Support

Our personality structure is built upon the foundation of our core wound. The core wound is that place in us where we feel like a total failure, a worthless impostor in our own life. Carrying a core wound does not mean we cannot be successful, happy with satisfying interpersonal relationships. It means that when we are in a quiet moment with ourselves, there is a secret inadequacy, a longing ache, in the solar plexus. We feel a combination of being both lost and unappreciated by ourselves and all others in our life.

We typically approach weakness and insecurity through *dukkha*—unsatisfactoriness. In life successes as well as life losses, we can find a tinge of unhappiness in the moments of great joy. Paying attention to these unhappy moments assists us in seeing the undercurrent of unsatisfactoriness that points toward the cause—the core wound.

Practicing with Weakness and Insecurity

We start approaching this feeling of weakness and insecurity by breathing into the solar plexus. We sense with our breath what is here in this moment. If you feel both an urge to leave and a sense that it is impossible to change, that is often a confirmation that you are in touch with that deep inadequacy or worthlessness. We feel inadequate and ineffectual—essentially, we are lost within ourselves. Likewise, we do not know exactly what to do or what steps to take. Our inner defenses have been activated, and we are contracting within in an act of protection.

We develop the ability and skill of being with these dark, uncomfortable places within by cautiously approaching. When the discomfort is too intense or overwhelming, we should back away and turn to our innate goodness meditation to contact the ever-present lightness, buoyancy, and connection with our deeper or true nature (see "Innate Goodness with I-Am-Not and I-Am Practices" in Chapter 1).

> *We want our contact with unsettled places within to be slightly uncomfortable, not unbearable. When our discomfort is paralyzing, we cannot engage the underlying issue.*

As we gain more buoyancy with our innate goodness meditation practice, we will increase our ability to be with inner unwanted places. The strategy is to come as close to your discomfort as is possible without actually being overwhelmed or bolting to escape the discomfort. We want our contact with unsettled places within to be slightly uncomfortable, not unbearable. When our discomfort is paralyzing, we cannot engage the underlying issue.

Breathe into the discomfort. Admit that feeling that you are already defeated. Feel the discomfort and the typical avoidant strategies you use when confronted by these core convictions. Do not engage with your avoidant strategies; just feel their presence, too. Should you start feeling overwhelmed, shift back to innate goodness practice to feel the unbroken connection with your authentic heart.

Breathing into the solar plexus, just be with whatever content or reaction is present. Try to hold the understanding that this discomfort is conditioned—that is, subject to change. It will, and must, change.

Feel your own weakness. Sense the self-belief that you are not capable, not competent to manage life. Let your body assume the posture of utter defeat. Feel the sense of inability. The posture may well appear hunched over, collapsing in on itself. Feel the body and muscle weakness that accompanies a sense of defeat. You may sense something like ice water in your arms and legs. Allow the emotions of sadness, anguish, and fear to be right here. You do not need to fully accept those emotional reactions. Just feel them as fully as is possible.

Draw upon your memories of failure, inability, or defeat. Recall the times you were deeply embarrassed or shamed by your failings.

Make contact with the belief of *I am convinced I am a failure, incapable, incompetent.* Feel into your belief, your conviction, your unquestioned confidence in this statement.

Feel the fullness of your history with these self-beliefs. Sense the discomfort and suffering engendered by them.

Shortly, a lightness will commence that is both a lightness of tone and a lessening of belief in your lack of self-worth. The beliefs will then not feel so unquestionably true. With time and repeated engagement, you will find a neutrality developing. This is not a form of numbness but rather deep acceptance.

> *As if by magic, a lightness, a goodness, a universal and objective love will be activated.*

Being deeply with the negative self-beliefs will tap off the energy we place in warning of adjacent difficult emotions and memories. The energy will lighten and not feel overwhelming. As if by magic, a lightness, a goodness, a universal and objective love will be activated. These sensations are not personal but objectively universal—the province of the Absolute, the source of all creation and manifestation.

JOURNALING

Weakness-and-Insecurity Exercise

Take a few moments to answer the following questions in your journal:

1 What is your lifetime history and experience with weakness and insecurity?
2 In what circumstances do weakness and insecurity arise?
3 How are weakness and insecurity helpful to you in your present life?

Weakness and Insecurity to Unconditioned Support

Many of us feel, and have felt, internal weakness of body and/or mind. Often with this perception of weakness is a mental insecurity. We feel incapable, unable to muster sufficient strength in a particular situation or in life in general. We need to develop the ability to be with the weakness and insecurity as fully as is possible. As you access these feelings, notice the ice water feeling in your arms and legs. Let yourself experience how it feels like too much effort to raise an arm or stand on your legs.

As we stay with the weakness and insecurity whenever they arise, separately or together, we begin to experience something that feels solid, immovable, within. This occurs when we are touching into the unconditioned support of the Absolute in our true nature.

In daily life, when we seek support from another person, we engage in a process of communication and possibly bargaining. This person may have needs that must be resolved before they can fully support us in our present dynamic. Over time their support might change or fade based upon their life demands and the nature of the relationship we are in. In short, even if we can mostly count on another person's commitment of emotional support, on some inner level we may expect they will not be able to sustain their offer.

Support of the Absolute is not conditional. This is a support we do not need to negotiate or bargain for. It is not dependent upon another's moods or whims. It does not fade when conditions change. It is always available to us.

The Absolute is available whenever we recognize the limitations of the personality to meet life's challenges.

The invitation of inner Absolute support begins with honestly meeting with and opening to feelings of overwhelm. We need to feel our inability to withstand what is happening. Accepting that you do not personally have the resources to support yourself is key. It is through this candid self-assessment that we begin to open to other responses or sources. In our surrender to the overwhelm, we send a message to the Absolute: *I am at my end. I have no resources available.*

The Absolute is available whenever we recognize the limitations of the personality to meet life's challenges. In this surrender, we unknowingly turn toward a solution provided by the Absolute. *I give up* is a powerful admission. In this opening, I can begin to feel or sense stability commence. It feels as though a foundation is arising under my feet. Suddenly, I have a ground that is supporting me. I then feel a solidity forming, particularly in support of my back. It is as though a formidable structure or wall appears to uphold me. From this growing connection and stability, I settle. My inner state becomes more constant and reliable. I can see the friction points more clearly. Response choices begin to appear that were out of view moments before. I know what to do! I am not lost!

Common Resistances to Unconditioned Support

Common resistances to welcoming unconditioned support include the conviction that we are unworthy and valueless, fear of being overwhelmed by unconditioned support, and fear of fully becoming authentic.

- Conviction we are unworthy and valueless: In the process of breaking the dual unity quality of our young lives, we blame ourselves for the break with Presence. We cannot blame the Absolute as it did nothing wrong. We feel we cannot blame our caregivers for the loss of unity with Presence because we so desperately need them for survival. The only person left to blame, in our young minds, is us

  We begin a self-identity story: If I were not bad, unlovable, worthless, helpless, hopeless, I would have maintained the unity with Presence. This is such a core story of identity we rarely question it. We hold it as an irrefutable universal law, like gravity.
- Fear of being overwhelmed by unconditioned support: As part of the process of being autonomous as a human, we, at strategic times, pull away from our caregivers. We test our new wings in a solo flight. Emotionally needy caregivers are triggered by the child's perceived

withdrawal, and, in response, they advance toward the child emotionally to fill in the growing gap between them. The child can feel this as an unwanted intrusion, an invasion that we might call "overmerging." If the caregiver acts in this way routinely, the child will have a reluctance toward merging with another. This attitude and perspective may be projected onto the Absolute. When unconditioned support appears in the individual's consciousness, they recoil from it. They will need to process the overmerging of their life and see what is true about the fear of overmerging and what is false. Whatever is outdated and false today must be released to support the flowering of truth.

— Fear of fully becoming authentic: In some cultures, there is a social message to not stand out. Self-promoting and focusing too much on yourself are behaviors outside the norms of these societies and are socially discouraged. The rare times when we do access our deepest, authentic self and carefully reveal it to another may become negative experiences if that person minimizes or judges us. This sends a message to us that we must protect—even hide—our true self or true nature from everyone, including ourselves. The result may be a fear of being authentic.

Resistances-to-Support Exercise

Take a few moments to answer the following questions in your journal:

1 What is your lifetime history and experience with these resistances?
2 In what circumstances do these resistances arise?
3 How are these resistances helpful to you in your present life?

My Experience with Weakness, Insecurity, and Unconditioned Support

As a child I was very introverted. I had a stutter and flushed red with embarrassment easily. I felt I was weak and extremely self-conscious. Every action or word I spoke was reflected upon afterward. I constantly found fault in my everyday living. I felt I was seriously lacking inner strength, confidence, and any level of support. Whenever I felt my insecurity, I contracted further within. I suspect I believed that if I could withdraw sufficiently, I would not be touched by my self-conscious insecurities. As you will suspect, this approach and this strategy were ineffectual.

My first step was fully admitting my weakness and self-conscious insecurity. I had to approach my perception of inner weakness with the compass of truth. The truth became more important than my fears of confirming my inner state of weakness. As I began to deliberately and knowingly approach and contact my self-beliefs and insecurities, I did so with the thirst for what was true. Even if I ultimately confirmed my weakness and insecurity, it was better to know the truth than to use distractions to avoid it.

Interestingly, as I opened to my weakness, I could see the pattern of neglect in my young life. I did not feel I had any support in my life. Regrettably, I was an unwanted child in my family. My parents' open disdain for me was overwhelming. My parents did not care for me. I was viewed mostly as a regrettable nuisance, so my only available resource was to try and disappear. This was true. As an adult, I approached my mother in a private one-on-one moment. I told her I felt she did not care for me or love me as I was growing up. She had had a few glasses of wine and was prone to blunt honesty when drinking. She confirmed she did not care much for me as a child and did not feel love for me. She said, "I am learning to love you as an adult."

Rather than be devastated by her admission, I was elated. This confirmed my child perceptions. Because it was true my parents did not care for me as a child, my response of weakness and insecurity was entirely warranted. I had done my best.

This confirmation of my perception allowed me to feel some inner strength. I could then admit my lack of perceived strength and support and move on to consider how I could access inner strength or confidence when I was routinely rejected by my parents.

With this clear lens of truth, I could then open to sense and feel what else was here. I began to feel a slight confidence growing in me. I was not doing anything. This confidence was spontaneously arising on its own. I also felt a sense of a floor or ground developing under me. Rather than feel like I was constantly dangling in midair, I had a ground, a place to stand up in my life.

A sense of structure, of inner support, began to arise. When I worked this territory of my self-beliefs, I began to feel like steel was infusing my spine. My posture began to straighten from the hunched-over, defeated position previously held. I could breathe deeply as my body began to sit upright with reliable stability.

> *I also felt a sense that an outer structure or*
> *foundation was holding me. It was as though*
> *I was leaning against a massive edifice,*
> *something like the Colosseum in Rome.*

I also felt a sense that an outer structure or foundation was holding me. It was as though I was leaning against a massive edifice, something like the Colosseum in Rome.

These sensations of inner and outer support were revolutionary to me. I had always had to use my willpower to feel any measure of internal or external support. The conclusion that I was born a failure was fading. Any belief in my incompetence was lightening. I could ask the question, *Is it true I am a failure?* The response was either a resounding *No* or a neutral unanswered question waiting for further experience to reach a conclusion. I was content to be right here, open and available for any response to arise.

Envy and Jealousy:
A Distortion of Empathetic Joy (*Mudita*)

Most of us grow up feeling that love and material possessions are in short supply. We never fully receive what we seek or want. We learn to live with the disappointment of lowered expectations.

When we see another have a success that we wish for, this can activate our envy or jealousy. Our envy and jealousy are linked to our life relationship to scarcity and abundance. How much needed emotional contact and how many important possessions do we feel are available to us?

Envy arises when we ache for another's success or good fortune to be ours. The other's success feels like our failure, like a loss. This ache can cause us to feel we will never get what we need. Envy is not just craving someone else's success; it stirs our conviction of our future losses.

Whereas in envy we witness *with sadness* another person receiving something that we want, in jealousy we also feel *anger* in this situation.

We all desire to be seen and treated as uniquely special. When we are in contact with our deeper nature, we know that there is enough for all. We can celebrate another's good fortune as if it is our own.

Practicing with Envy and Jealousy

To contact your envy and jealousy, begin by recalling a memory from your past. You are looking for a memory where you really wanted something (a certain score on a test, a job promotion, a romantic partner, or some possession). Remember when you did not get that desired item? How did it feel?

If you experienced envy, it may have felt like a deep longing for that particular object of desire. Jealousy is quite similar but has a flavor of anger in it. In jealousy we are angry that the other person received our object of desire.

One psychological effect we can experience with envy or jealousy is a confirmation that our personality, our personhood, was insufficient to receive the object of desire. In other words, we conclude we are so meaningless to others in our life that we are overlooked or passed over.

Envy-and-Jealousy Exercise

Take a few moments to answer the following questions in your journal:

1   What is your lifetime history and experience with envy and jealousy?
2   In what circumstances do envy and jealousy arise?
3   How are envy and jealousy helpful to you in your present life?

Envy and Jealousy to Empathetic Joy

Empathetic joy, called *mudita* in Pali, is the joy we feel at another's success, happiness, or joy. In *mudita,* another's joy or success feels literally indistinguishable from our joy or success.

In practicing with empathetic joy, we learn to relax and surrender our envy and jealousy by seeing experientially how the Absolute functions in the world as freely abundant and available without restriction, limit, or measure. Learning to trust the Absolute's abundance, we feel open to celebrating whenever we witness another in the joy of receiving.

Common Resistances to Empathetic Joy

Some resistances to empathetic joy include a lifetime of fear of scarcity; conviction that if we open to empathetic joy, it will confirm we are not worthy or valued; and the belief that if we open to empathetic joy, it will be taken away immediately.

— Fear of scarcity: Many young lives experience a lack of love or material possessions. We conclude that there simply is not enough love or material possessions to ensure we get what we feel is an adequate supply. We are resigned to that reality. This fear of a shortage or scarcity can be activated whenever we see another receive love or material possessions or when we find ourselves longing. Through repeated contact with the

Absolute and its unconditioned, nonconceptual nature, we develop more confidence that the Absolute and our life are actually plentiful.

- Conviction that if we open to empathetic joy, it will confirm we are not worthy or valued: Some people resist receiving joy or possessions because we feel unworthy and believe there is a strong possibility that the other will withdraw their gifts when they discover the truth of our core wound. These people may also worry that when they see another receive love or possessions, their underlying belief in a lack of self-worth will be revealed by their jealousy or envy, and they will be rejected. For this reason, they resist feeling joy for another. Through repeated contact with empathetic joy, this self-belief anchored in the core wound will be lovingly challenged, loosened, and dropped.

- Belief that if we open to empathetic joy, it will be taken away immediately: Growing up, we may have had emotionally volatile caregivers whose moods could not be anticipated. Our experience may have included the hasty withdrawal of the love or possessions we were seeking if we asked at the seemingly wrong time. With repeated contact with the Absolute, we come to know and trust its offerings, which are given without qualifications and never withdrawn. It is always the human who, feeling emotionally rejected by the Absolute, turns away from it.

Resistances-to-Empathetic-Joy Exercise

Take a few moments to answer the following questions in your journal:

1 What is your lifetime history and experience with these resistances?
2 In what circumstances do these resistances arise?
3 How are these resistances helpful to you in your present life?

My Experience with Envy, Jealousy, and Empathetic Joy

My belief as a child was that love and possessions were rarely offered and quickly withdrawn if I did not accept them in an expected or predicted manner.

Also, being from a large family, I felt that others routinely received more than I did. Whether this favoritism was true or not is irrelevant. I felt it to be true and felt resentment accordingly.

These beliefs led me to a complicated, tenuous relationship to joy and success. I fully believed that if another received love or possessions, I would receive less love and fewer possessions. Thus, I was fairly incapable of truly being happy for another. I witnessed the other's joy as my failure and loss. This sense of failure could activate my survival instincts and leave me panicking that not only was there not enough but also that I might lose possessions I had on hand.

With the perception and experience of the complete Oneness of *kenshō*, I witnessed the magnitude and generosity of the Absolute. Each being is held as uniquely special in the same objective love and tenderness as all the other beings. While I was not more special than another, I was witnessed and tenderly held as incredibly special by the Absolute. I was the expression of the Absolute. The Absolute is profoundly unique and beneficial to all equally.

> *There is, in reality, always a surplus of both love
> and possessions in the world. My perspective was
> the limiting factor.*

This *satori* experience of seeing deeply into true nature
allowed me to start seeing love and possessions as an undivided quantity. There is, in reality, always a surplus of both
in the world. My perspective was the limiting factor. Once
that was revealed to be erroneous and then corrected, I
could easily rejoice at another's success or happiness.

Guilt: A Distortion of Loving-Kindness (*Mettā*)

On our spiritual journey, from First Awakening to fully
integrated self-realization, we must be oriented inward. We
must become intimate with and adept at navigating our
interiority of experience. This inner turn can feel disquiet-
ing. It can feel like we are rejecting our life, our loves, and
our world and abandoning our humanness. In effect, we are
temporarily doing just that. Yet this necessary turning away
is actually not a rejection of exterior life. Remarkably, as we
turn inward, we come into greater contact and connection
with the exterior world. When I went through this process,
I realized that the more I turned inward, the more engaged

and connected I felt in the outside world. My life made more sense as I was more authentic in my actions and behavior.

However, the experience of happiness or gratification can trigger guilt that others are not able to enjoy these same pleasures. We may feel selfish or self-centered because we are taking care of ourselves and not attending to the many issues of the world. When the guilt couples with the witnessing of another's suffering, it does not afford us sufficient interior space for loving-kindness to arise. We need to recognize, and be present to, our guilt as it arises. Under observation, guilt moves from unconsciousness to consciousness. The act of seeing it reduces its effect on us. Guilt, when witnessed, can become something we can engage rather than something that overwhelms us.

Practicing with Guilt

Recall a memory where you felt a guilt or shame reaction or response. Notice where in your body the feeling of guilt is still active. Approach the guilt as gently as possible. Often people will feel a sense of inner collapse when meeting inner guilt or shame. If collapse is here for you, let yourself feel it as fully as possible. Is it helpful to let your body assume the posture of guilt or shame? Notice how you feel little, small, insignificant when touching into guilt or shame.

Guilt Exercise

Take a few moments to answer the following
questions in your journal:

1 What is your lifetime history and experience
   with guilt?
2 In what circumstances does guilt arise?
3 How is guilt helpful to you in your present life?

Guilt to Loving-Kindness

Guilt is a common experience for most people. Whenever our psychological structure of the inner critic or superego is activated by our making a mistake, guilt and/or shame can arise. The superego's function is to correct us while trying to make us feel small and weak.

By openly accepting the guilt without taking it personally, we soften. We can realize that guilt is a reaction of mind. By being willing to be with our guilt, we soften and invite tenderness and love. As we welcome tenderness and love, we become more and more tender ourselves. Through more fully accepting and being with our tender love, we open to the unborn love, the loving-kindness of the Absolute.

Developing and inviting loving-kindness toward another is a light, open, unencumbered connection. It is generous of heart and free of any clinging or egoic stickiness.

Usually translated as "loving-kindness," *mettā* meditation provides a way to meet the challenges of painful life experiences with openhearted love. Feeling into loving and kindness, we sense a particular support, an enduring lightness that is inherent. This is the loving lightness we need to meet life challenges and struggles with an open heart.

Developing and inviting loving-kindness toward another is a light, open, unencumbered connection. It is generous of heart and free of any clinging or egoic stickiness. Stickiness is that compulsion to grab something desired. It is usually messy and poorly executed due to our extreme neediness. When the warmheartedness of loving-kindness is filtered through our personality patterning and our places of hurt, it may reveal our underlying neediness. This neediness confirms we are wanting recognition, validation, or appreciation from another to feel good about ourselves. Emotional neediness lacks the stability and freedom of loving-kindness. By "freedom," I mean that the love is freely given without consideration of any return. It is open, spacious, and unrestricted.

Common Resistances to Loving-Kindness

There are a number of well-known resistances to loving-kindness, including aversion and self-hatred.

— Aversion: When we meet unwanted, painful experiences, one popular response is aversion. Aversion is a sweeping rejection of what is happening now, and it allows us to hide from or avoid reality. The rationale behind this is that when we can suppress the pain of life, we will have only pleasant, pleasurable experiences. But this does not work. We are only temporarily masking the emotional suffering, and it will probably still be here after our aversion wanes. If we commit to aversion as an avoidant life strategy, we unknowingly narrow connection with our hearts. Aversion strategies serve only to wall off our hearts and to limit our contact with and impressionability to the warm, melting tenderness of loving-kindness.

- Self-hatred: Each of us has internalized our early caregivers' criticism of us. As children, our very survival can feel dependent upon agreeing with the criticism directed toward us. We may see our caregiver as perfect and feel we are deeply flawed in comparison. Sometimes we join in their negative judgment of us to temper the sting of their rejection. If we keep up this behavior long enough, it becomes an unchallenged belief, despite the suffering we feel. If we accept their criticism, it can smolder into ongoing, unconscious self-criticism, even self-hatred. When we are enmeshed in self-hatred or self-judgment, we close our connection to our heart. We do not welcome the openheartedness needed for the arising of loving-kindness.

Resistances-to-Loving-Kindness Exercise

Take a few moments to answer the following questions in your journal:

1 What is your lifetime history and experience with these resistances?
2 In what circumstances do these resistances arise?
3 How are these resistances helpful to you in your present life?

My Experience with Guilt and Loving-Kindness (Unborn Love)

I was a child with a fairly developed superego. It was an internalized parental figure for me. Any trivial or minute mistake would trigger a superego response of deep disappointment, self-identification as a failure, and abject surrender. I learned to run, quickly, from any guilt triggers or reactions.

As my meditation practice and spiritual one-on-one work with teachers progressed, I was able to learn to be present, to be open, to my guilt. I learned that I could acknowledge I had made a mistake without it resulting in an unfixable error and confirming my self-perception as an abject failure.

As I was able to be with my guilt more openly, I felt a tenderness, a care, a love seeping through the inner cracks in my guilt.

Through these cracks in my inner facade, I was able to feel authentic unborn love of *mettā*. "Unborn" refers to the unconditioned quality. Anything unborn has no birth, decay, or death.

Greed and Resentment: A Distortion of Equanimity (*Upekkhā*)

Resentment is an angry, even bitter, rejecting of the present moment when we feel we have been treated unfairly. There is an internal conclusion that what is occurring is unwelcome. Typically, we reject events that do not reflect our sense of self in the world. This rejection is fueled when we are not seen as our cherished self-image. When this occurs, we respond to what is happening with an angry rejection of reality.

Greed is an unquenchable thirst for more. It is a yearning that compulsively reaches for whatever we think will make us whole, happy, and complete. It is a thirst for greater admiration, increased recognition, and more possessions to try to fill our neediness. This greed comes from our firm belief in our self-deficiency.

Practicing with Greed and Resentment

It is best to start with the most vivid memory of greed that can be recalled. Pick a time when you desperately wanted someone or something, when your desire was nearly uncontrollable. You *had* to have it no matter the cost. Sense into and feel the inner hunger, the ache of wanting. Notice how desperate you feel in this memory. Can you feel the qualities of greed and desperation in your present-moment experience? Where in your body are they located?

To engage with resentment, we search for a memory in which we deeply resented a particular situation, dynamic, or person. This is a memory where you will find anger and disgust. You may find some qualities of rage in the memory also. Feel deeply into the memory, dropping the content of the memory to feel the underlying resentment. It can feel like an ongoing, gnawing anger at events that are not to your liking.

Greed-and-Resentment Exercise

Take a few moments to answer the following questions in your journal:

1 What is your lifetime history and experience with greed and resentment?
2 In what circumstances do greed and resentment arise?
3 How are greed and resentment helpful to you in your present life?

Greed and Resentment to Equanimity

Our ongoing resistances to greed and resentment block our ability to sense and feel these emotions fully. Because we have social and familial judgments that good people do not feel greed or resentment, we may attempt a spiritual bypass when these and other unwanted emotions and reactions are present. By "spiritual bypass," I mean turning to deep meditation or transcendent experience in avoidance of the unwanted, rejected emotions.

> *We begin to see that the goal of spiritual practice and engagement is not maintaining any particular state or spiritual quality—it is* accurately and wholesomely being with whatever is present in this moment.

In normalizing these and other unwanted emotions, we begin to see that the goal of spiritual practice and engagement is not maintaining any particular state or spiritual quality—it is *accurately and wholesomely being with whatever is present in this moment.* When we are openly present with these challenging emotions, the energy from the event that is embedded in these emotions is released or tapped off. The energy lessens. As the energy dissipates, we can more easily make deeper contact with the emotion and the underlying trigger. Often the underlying trigger for greed and resentment is a deep yearning, a desirous wanting that typically cannot be satisfied.

By being with the truth of these emotions and the underlying hunger, we orient toward deeply accepting the presence of the wanting, the hunger of isolation we are trying to fill, and we can fully accept the entire content of this present moment. Accepting the truth of this moment is the practice and presentation of equanimity.

> *Equanimity generates a quality of trust in our hearts that we are exactly in the right place at the right time.*

Equanimity is a feeling of perfect balance. Everything that is occurring inside or outside of us is exactly right in this moment. Equanimity generates a quality of trust in our hearts that we are exactly in the right place at the right time. It empowers us to possess a level of acceptance, of balanced perspective, for the objective, universal truth that is always here with us. We open our awareness, our consciousness, to equanimity as a manifestation of the Absolute by orienting toward ultimate reality, unadorned truth.

It is important to distinguish equanimity from indifference, which can look similar. Indifference is a psychological numbing to anticipated pain, suffering, or dissatisfaction with life. We may feel we must reconcile ourselves to experiencing repeated disappointment, which leads to a surrender of not caring. Indifference is a strategy we use to block the pain of life's lack of value for who we are. If we numb ourselves, we believe we are protected from any misattunement with others.

One crucial difference between indifference and equanimity is acceptance. With equanimity, there is a deep acceptance of what is happening, and there is minimal effort to control an outcome. Equanimity and indifference also *feel* distinct; indifference is a suppressing of your vitality, while with equanimity there is an open, warm felt sense of a rightness about life as it is unfolding.

Common Resistances to Equanimity

Some of the common resistances to equanimity include a rejection of this moment and fear that life contains nearly exclusively bad results.

— Rejection of this moment: According to brain researchers, most people today focus about 90 percent of their attention on a combination of the past and the future. That leaves about 10 percent of our attention focused on this moment. This moment is the only moment of reality. There is no other measure of time. Terms like "past" and "future" are concepts only. When we abide in the past, usually working remorse and regret issues, or when we invest in planning the future to avoid negative experiences, we are not here, in the eternal now.

We avoid the present moment because it is crackling with aliveness. It is a little too real. We can feel a reticence, a reluctance to fully be present with the energy of aliveness. We feel more contained and controlled when we work with thought-concepts of past or future. We feel safer. One of the important benefits of equanimity is acceptance—true, unrestrained acceptance—of the events that are happening in real time in this very moment.

- Fear that life contains nearly exclusively bad results: Sometimes life does not unfold in a way we secretly envisioned. Sometimes we get exactly what we expected, but it fades much too soon. These experiences leave us with a certain distrust in life. We come to believe not only that if we want something, we will be disappointed by not getting it, but also that our life could worsen if we do get it. With this perspective and mindset, we are mostly closed to the truth of this moment.

Resistances-to-Equanimity Exercise

Take a few moments to answer the following questions in your journal:

1   What is your lifetime history and experience with these resistances?
2   In what circumstances do these resistances arise?
3   How are these resistances helpful to you in your present life?

My Experience with Greed, Resentment, and Equanimity

As I discussed earlier, because I was one of the younger children in an extended family, I often felt a less-than-full member of the group. I felt, rightly or wrongly, that my older siblings received more attention, love, and understanding than I did. I felt my parents had a strong preference for the older siblings. This led to a feeling of greed whenever an opportunity for my parents' attention arose. During those rare moments, I would grab on to their attention and try my best to sustain their interest. Whenever my parents paid attention to my older and younger siblings, I felt resentful. Why did it seem to be such a challenge for my parents to attend and attune to me? Why did it appear more effortless when they attended to my siblings?

I struggled with my feelings and beliefs about this difficult family dynamic for a long time until I finally accepted it. Once I could accept the objective fact—the objective reality—that my parents preferred my siblings to me, I could fully exhale. I could feel relief. What I witnessed was objectively true. Rather than a crushing admission, it was a liberation from all the conflicting and competing thoughts I had had while trying to avoid the conclusion that my parents did not like me very much.

The underlying inner fear that we will confirm the worst is what keeps us from accepting truth. Once we can accept the truth of our deep longing, our wanting to be loved and included, we can more fully accept the truth of how life actually is rather than holding on to our deepest wish for how life should be.

My first deep contact with equanimity as a meditation practice was in the two-month retreat with my Theravada Buddhist teacher. I became intimate with equanimity not only through the breath awareness *jhāna* practice but also through a stand-alone concentration meditation practice of the *brahmavihāras*, or ancient Buddhist heart practices.

I recall the first deep experience of equanimity. I was looking at a fallen tree near where I was staying during the retreat. A squirrel had gotten entwined in the fallen tree and died. I could feel the destructive side of life yet also feel a balance and appropriateness. Everything in life was exactly in the right place regardless of whether that place matched my idea of the right place. Perfect imperfection was the experience. Nothing needed to be removed or added despite the lack of worldly perfection. This was a deep acceptance of the relative imperfection of the Absolute in our world of form and name, the form world. I was witnessing the unconditioned manifesting in the conditioned world before me.

Cruelty: A Distortion of Compassion (*Karuṇā*)

To fully engage the path of Awakening and functioning self-realization, we must—I repeat, *must*—be able to be with all aspects and expressions of our psychology. We will not progress to the deeper, more realized experiences unless we can wade into what feels like our personal swamp, our rejected and disowned parts.

You may have an early memory of taking quiet, secret delight in another's suffering. It may have been someone who previously hurt you. Perhaps after they hurt you, you witnessed them undergo something painful. Maybe you felt a little glee seeing this. Maybe you even said something that added to their suffering. Intentionally making another's suffering worse is cruelty.

When you take pleasure in the suffering of a person you dislike or hate, you are suspending the spontaneous arising of compassion. We need to honestly and courageously wade into the discomfort of our past hurtful behaviors to be fully open to compassion. As we learn to reveal and recognize our cruelty, we are less driven by it on a subconscious level. Cruelty can then become a conscious choice, and when that happens, it can also be abandoned. This turning from cruelty helps us open to the presence of gentle compassion.

Practicing with Cruelty

Whenever a student is seeing or meeting life issues that suggest cruelty is a psychological issue for them, I have them orient toward a memory of cruelty. This can usually be revealed by recalling a horrible argument with a romantic partner. Most people, I find, have had at least one relationship that was tumultuous. Cruelty in argument is when you feel and perceive that your partner said something that felt like a deep cut. Often when a partner speaks to us in a manner we find cruel, their words leave a psychological and emotional papercut. Our typical response is to come up with a remark that is equally or more hurtful than what we experienced. Virtually everyone can recall this type of memory.

I suggest that my student rests awareness in that memory and recalls how it felt before they responded with the cruel remark. The desire to wound the other is often the felt sense. The hurtful words are also imbued with a certain type of glee that the person will feel wounded by us.

Cruelty Exercise

Take a few moments to answer the following
questions in your journal:

1 What is your lifetime history and experience
   with cruelty?
2 In what circumstances does cruelty arise?
3 How is cruelty helpful to you in your present life?

Cruelty to Compassion

Once we can acknowledge that we are capable of cruelty under the right circumstances, and once we accept the times in our life when we have chosen to be cruel, we can become more authentic in our emotional life. We can accept our human frailty by acknowledging that each of us carries the potential for harmful behavior or action. This lets us settle more into the truth of who we are, while relaxing our sense of who we take ourselves to be. Instead of being fixated on an ideal self-image, we can be more honest to ourselves and therefore to others in our world.

As we soften our protective psychological shell, we can allow more of the world to reach over and touch our interiority. We can more readily feel the pain, the suffering, the *dukkha* as we Buddhists call it. By feeling our suffering without avoidance or minimization, we can open more authentically to the Absolute and invite the Absolute quality of compassion (*karuṇā*).

Navigating these difficult areas, we need to have tenderness and compassion for ourselves.

On our journey of spiritual Awakening and embodiment, we will pass through many familiar areas of our history, memories, and psyche that remain painful. Yet the light of objective, universal truth beckons us closer to our tender places. Navigating these difficult areas, we need to have tenderness and compassion for ourselves.

Compassion is often misapplied in Buddhist practice. Many Buddhists believe that the function of compassion is to *take away* painful life events. This is not compassion's full benefit. Using compassion in our meditative practices provides gentle support, a kindhearted holding that allows us, and others, to be with our pain and persevere.

Compassion helps us draw closer to an enduring truth that is very different from the subjective truth that supports the story of our lives. In our life narratives, we cast ourselves in a particular role, typically that of the good, pure, innocent one. With sustained *karuṇā* practice, we begin to see that we maintain this young, pure, innocent self-image to present to others as the source of our pain, and we are confronted by the universal truth that we encompass many emotions and levels of identity.

Compassion assists us in developing the ability to be with *whatever* state of mind or emotion is present. When we are not seeking exclusively good experiences and instead feel what is authentically present, we are drawn closer to the truth of our Beingness.

It is important to distinguish compassion from pity, which can look similar. When we pity someone, we are observing them with superiority. We are witnessing their suffering from an emotional, elevated distance. We may feel bad for them, yet we cannot offer authentic support when we are anchored in pity. We see the person we pity as a victim. We almost believe they might deserve this suffering. Pity is not supportive or kind but judgmental and often condescending.

Our righteous anger on behalf of someone who is suffering is not compassion either. Like pity, righteous anger originates from an inner sense of superiority. It feels unquestionably right. We *know* what is best for everyone. When another does not behave or act in the way we think is best, their actions can trigger our anger. We are not offering support that helps the hurting person be with their pain. Instead, in righteous anger we may be attacking the cause of the pain.

Common Resistances to Compassion

Some of the common resistances to compassion include habitual hard- or closed-heartedness and fear of being con-firmed forever weak and dependent.

— Habitual hard- or closed-heartedness: One learned life strategy for avoiding discomfort or pain is to close ourselves, principally our heart, to anything we perceive as negative or harmful. This appears to be a wise choice at first blush. In closing our heart, we feel we are pro-tecting its vulnerability. The typical impact of closing our hearts is that we become weaker internally. Because our heart does not have the opportunity to expand and contract in response to the authentic conditions of life, we do not develop the suppleness that is essential in deep meditative practice. For this reason, much of the *brahmavihāras* practice is a process of tenderizing us to ourselves and opening our hearts to receive the Absolute.

— Fear of being confirmed forever weak and dependent: It is a common internal understanding that to be dependent is to be weak. If we need others, we are open to their neglect or withdrawal of support. Since many of us have experienced ongoing or continuous neglect, we have learned to expect it, and plan for it, in the normal course of life. We strive for autonomy and independence. We feel *If I can be self-sustaining, I will not be dependent, I will not be weak, I will not be vulnerable. I will be completely safe.*

In order to open to compassion, we need to be willing to be authentically vulnerable. We need to *not* know the answer or solution to the problem of life. We need to be an empty, willing vessel ready to receive.

Resistances-to-Compassion Exercise

Take a few moments to answer the following
questions in your journal:

1   What is your lifetime history and experience
    with these resistances?
2   In what circumstances do these resistances arise?
3   How are these resistances helpful to you in your
    present life?

My Experience with Cruelty and Compassion

In my earlier life, I saw myself as only good and innocent. I could recast and rewrite reality to find justification for my behavior. Due to this distorted self-belief, I gave myself permission in my younger years to be hurtful and cruel to others, without remorse or regret. Since I was an expert at finding an innocent motivation for all of my actions, I could never acknowledge wrongdoing or mistake.

As I began working with the full Zen precepts (see Appendix) decades ago, and as truth became the most important compass of my life and spiritual practice, I had to admit to myself that I hurt people's feelings at times, either intentionally or with a disregard for the impact of my words and actions. Once I could admit my penchant for cruelty, I could atone for my thoughts and actions. This afforded me some inner softening of my self-identity. As I softened internally, I could feel the tenderheartedness, sensitivity, and openness I was protecting with cruelty. I could feel that inner pain. Touching into my inner pain allowed me to realize I did not have the inner resources to hold my pain and discomfort. I had to seek help from outside myself. This led to me opening to the Absolute in a moment of pure surrender, admitting I was lost and seeking some support. The support arrived as tenderhearted compassion. It felt like incredibly strong, gentle hands holding my inner wounds in such a way that I was not motivated to lash out at others. I could stay with my hurt place with heartful tenderness.

For many of my early years as a meditation student, I believed and acted as though compassion meant eliminating or fixing my or another's problem(s). In effect, this understanding and behavior perpetuate a righteous savior mentality. In other words, it is now our job to save ourselves and others from the slightest discomfort or pain. Needless to say, this approach did not work. I learned a lot about how to distract myself or another from discomfort, yet I did not learn how to be openly unguarded with the *dukkha*, the discomfort of human life. Some of the most important life and spiritual lessons are accessed by abiding in and inhabiting our discomfort and pain.

I saw this in real time when I was trying to help prevent one of my children from making what I considered to be a major life mistake. I was able to curtail the progression of their discomfort and pain. I slowed or stopped their eventual collapse.

In the midst of my inner celebration about what a wonderful person and father I was, I witnessed my child make an even worse choice than the one I had just prevented, and I understood that they did so because I had meddled in the first difficulty. This was a deep learning of the importance of being with the pain without trying to remove, minimize, or excise it.

Remaining present to our discomfort and pain allows us to fully feel them, to let them teach us their important lessons, and to fully receive the tenderness of the Absolute.

"A lightning bolt permanently taking away false concepts"

One evening after a forgiveness practice in the meditation hall with Mugen Sensei, the mind turned sincere and honest. While washing my hands before going to bed, I had a moment when I looked at my hands and had a deep sense that I wanted to go down that road, the road to find the truth; nothing else felt more important than the truth. This urgency and intention I think came from the forgiveness practice earlier that day. This practice seemed to have a deep impact on me, especially with regard to people and beings I had hurt and also those that I had not yet forgiven and with whom I was therefore still angry.

When going to bed, I had a very deep but rather short episode where I felt incredibly sorry that I had hurt people and beings in my life. These were memories that had surfaced in the forgiveness practice earlier that day. I felt a deep sense of feeling sorry and that I must and will change. After this episode I felt that I never wanted to hurt anyone ever again and that I was now willing to change my life accordingly. This was so overwhelming and led to a psychological breakdown and confusion as to what to do about it and who I was.

I did not sleep long before I woke up because many odd things started to happen. I saw vivid visions and I had different kinds of experiences throughout the night. Some things

I experienced were very beautiful and creative; some were slightly unsettling.

During one startling moment, when I looked within, I could not find myself at all. Internally, my sense of self was just blank when I tried to recall who I was. I did not know what just happened, so I read Mugen Sensei's book *Demystifying Awakening*, and I then realized that it must have been a *satori* experience. Later that morning my teacher Mugen Sensei explained *satori* experiences and also calmed me down a bit by helping me realize I could still function and also remember my life, my name, my friends and family, etc.

Some things I could not locate were my self, feelings of my self, and a lot of emotions that I had previously taken as true and real. When I tried to recall, feel, or remember these things, there was just an odd and utter blankness in response. The way to deal with this was simply to not try to find my self and these emotions. It turned out that I could function much better without all these things!

After this experience, the body was very stressed. I experienced a rushing heart, and I could not really sleep well for a couple of days. The mind, though—the mind was beautiful, clear, and absolutely wonderful. Yes, the mind was probably very stressed, trying to figure out what had happened, but it was also very beautiful. It was such a relief, but at the same time a lot to get used to! My view of my personality had completely changed. I could no longer refer to my old sense of self, simply because I could not locate it. In this sense I did not have a choice of going back, even if, for some odd reason, I would have wanted to.

The weeks after the *satori* experience were mixed with wonderful, loving moments and experiences, and a strong and quite hard pull back to where I could feel emotional and mental suffering based on my previous life, and countless negative memories. After the *satori* experience, there was, and still is, a lot of work, trying to adjust behavior to match what is felt inside.

It's hard to explain the permanent relief following this experience. To put it plainly, it feels like suffering has gone down by a tremendous amount. There is so much less worry and fewer negative or sticky emotions compared to what comes with the territory when holding to a personality view. With less self-referencing, what is observed is seen more clearly. There is less conceptualizing going on, adding less of a filter through the personality structure to what is observed. The sense of awareness and presence is increased. I do not suffer so much anymore from drowsiness or sleepiness I had experienced as long as I can remember. But to say that all is very well is also not true. Because observations are tuned more clearly now, there is a lot of work to do adjusting one's life accordingly, to really investigate what beliefs one wants to let go of and what aspects one wants to keep.

If the previous *kenshō* experience was like a lovely experience of opening up to a curiosity as to what we are, then the *satori* experience was more like a lightning bolt that permanently took away a lot of false concepts all at once, including the very view of one's own personality, my personality.

| —STUDENT 3

"Completely accepted and merged into a love that suffused everything"

The narrative of this second Awakening experience begins when I had been wrestling with my first *kōan*—Mu—for roughly three weeks. Periods when it constantly preoccupied me, even off the cushion, alternated with periods when I found myself coming back to it more sporadically.

During one such more sporadic phase, I was in the middle of something of a difficult moment. My wife had just left for a work trip of several weeks, and I was facing a substantial period of solitude. At the same time, I discovered that I had made an administrative mistake with my previous year's tax residency and might have to pay a significantly higher tax rate than anticipated. I felt afraid of the financial consequences of this mistake and bad about myself for having made the error. I tried to deal with these emotions by sitting with them. When they became too intense, I asked for help, a kind of prayer directed out into the void: *Please show me the way through this*. Where the intuition to ask for help in this way came from I do not know—I have not prayed since I was a child—but its efficacy far exceeded any expectations that I held.

After roughly half an hour I found energy moving up from my lower stomach toward my head in powerful currents. The energy was neither pleasant nor unpleasant; I just let it move. As more and more energy moved, I found myself becoming more and more relaxed. Negative thought loops slowed down and eventually ceased. The contraction in my midsection eased. Something much closer to pure Presence became my reality.

This persisted for perhaps a day and a half. I continued with the activities of my daily life, but with a great sense of peace and a minimal sense of agency or self-positioning. I had not been thinking of my *kōan* at all, until one evening, while doing something in the kitchen, I did. All at once the answer seemed to surge up out of the ground all around me, with a clarity and obviousness that were utterly undeniable. In an instant that contained everything, I saw that there was nothing other than this, that anything apart from the pure existence of the instant was just conceptual, imaginary, subject to doubt. This was an awesome experience, in the religious sense of the word. There was awe in the positive sense at the scopeless scale of the thing, certainly, but a terror came with it as well, a terror rooted in the sudden realization that the solidity I had attributed to my beliefs about the world, about what I was, about what other people were, was entirely illusory. As this experience deepened and unfolded, I began to feel increasingly untethered from the conceptual orienting pillars of my existence, and I had moments of real fear of insanity, of truly losing touch with conventional reality.

I awoke the next morning feeling a powerful anxiety regarding my wife's absence and the concern that I was going through an extremely powerful and destabilizing experience in a relatively isolated situation. (We live in a comparatively rural setting just outside of a small city, and I work from home.) Too agitated to do anything else, I went for a walk in the forest, touching the anxiety in my chest and midsection with my awareness to the extent that was tolerable. Doing circuits of a forest path, I felt the sensations become less intense with every loop. I began to understand that the suffering I was experiencing was not actually related to my wife's absence in this moment but rather related to the extent of my attachment to her presence in my life, and to the unbearable but unavoidable reality that we would eventually be parted from each other, one way or another. I experienced the suffering as the energetic potential that would eventually be released when I would have to let my wife go, and the magnitude of that pain seemed without end.

As I continued to walk, a fascinating change in the suffering began to occur. The focus around my wife began to soften and started to broaden. It occurred to me that most everyone who has ever lived has been attached to people of comparable importance in their lives, whose loss they also need to deal with sooner or later. *And if I can feel this amount of suffering in the circumstances of my really quite privileged, secure, and comfortable existence*, it further occurred to me, *what must it be like to suffer acutely from some of the worst conditions that the world can produce? What must it be like to live in a war zone, to be a refugee separated from one's family in*

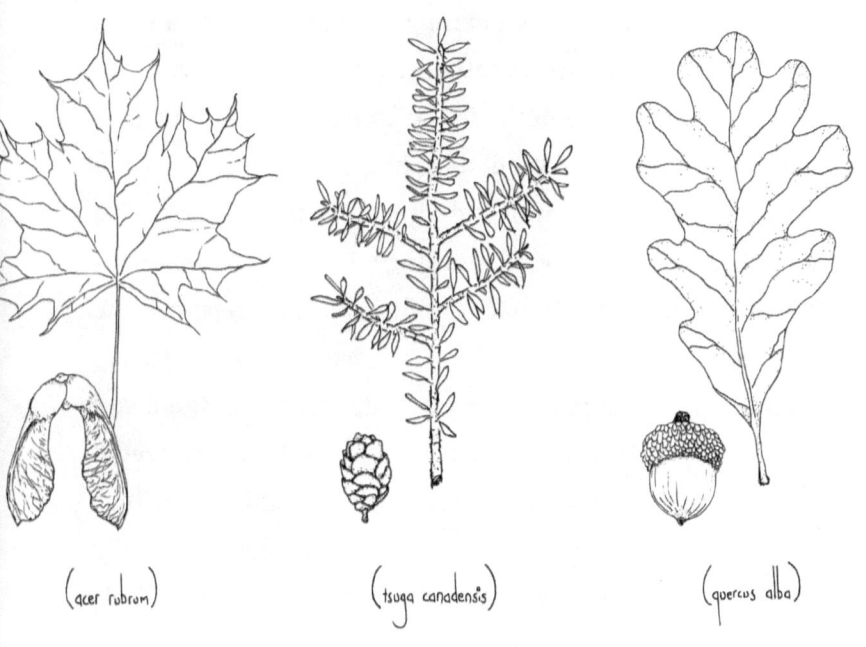

(acer rubrum)   (tsuga canadensis)   (quercus alba)

fear of one's life, to be a victim of systematic abuse, etc., etc. . . . ?
While this sounds like an intellectual chain of reasoning,
the experience was thoroughly intuitive, and I felt myself
opening by degrees to the infinite reality of the suffering
that suffuses existence. The line between my suffering and
the suffering of others became increasingly indistinct.

The intensity of this opening peaked and diminished,
and I returned home eventually, finally able to resume,
gently, some normal activities. Watching a film later that
evening, I found myself bursting into floods of tears at the
smallest representation of suffering and had to turn it off. I
awoke again the following morning with a comparable sensation of fear in my chest and midsection. As I repeated the
process of walking in the forest, the experience eventually
diminished to the point that I was able to come home and
sit with it. Intuitively I understood this fear to be connected
with sensations from early childhood, specifically feelings
of having been without agency, of having been repeatedly
forced to do many things that I did not want to do. This
part of myself clearly needed comfort and reassurance, and
I attempted to bring these qualities to bear as best I could,
essentially doing *mettā* for this part of my young self. Then
just as on the previous day, the experience of the fear began
to shift. I intuitively understood the fear to be coming from
successively younger and younger versions of myself, until it
became the consuming and primal fear of an infant, utterly
vulnerable, completely at the mercy of everything around

him, experiencing nothing in his preconceptual mind but animal/primal terror. I have trouble conveying how overwhelming and unendurable this experience felt.

With it, though, came the intuition that this primal experience of pain and fear and its repression is the universal foundation of ego and separation. The consequence of this was the uncovering of a radical, totally complete compassion. Experiencing this in the most unmediated form I ever had, I became immediately convinced that I could never blame another human for any negative action ever again. Confronted with the scale and enormity of the pain and fear that lie at the root of personal identity, I saw how even the most heinous acts become comprehensible. The line between my suffering and the suffering of others had disappeared completely. My experience rather felt like the suffering of the world: inexhaustible, terrible, unendurable.

It was at this point that I realized that I could not do this alone, and I reached out to Mugen Sensei and another spiritual friend. I needed help. This realization, mundane though it sounds, was significant. I became conscious that I had subtly been holding onto the idea that Awakening was something I would accomplish by myself, individualistically, through my own efforts and abilities. To this point in my life of practice, I had been very strong on the Buddha and the Dharma, but I had treated the Saṅgha, and the support of others, as an optional extra. Merely acknowledging that I had gotten into something far too big and powerful for the personality to contend with on its own amounted to a form of surrender and immediately brought a great sense of relief, as well as a critical shift in the trajectory of the unfolding.

My muscles, which throughout the fear experience had been tense and sore, began to relax and then relaxed some more. The knot in my lower stomach gradually dissolved; a profound peace slowly washed over me, slowly intensified. Discursive thoughts faded. Everything but the bare sense of perception faded. My reality blinked out of existence and back in, only once, unspectacularly. When it returned, I can only describe the feeling as my sins having been washed clean, to use the Christian terminology, as if those aspects of experience that I had been carrying around for as long as I remember—that felt subtly (or sometimes not so subtly) defective, fundamentally wrong or shameful—had been completely accepted and merged into a love that suffused everything, that was everything, powerful beyond imagination.

Many other interesting experiences followed. I understood for the first time what it means to experience the teacher's consciousness as one's own, for example, and traditions of guru yoga began to make sense to me in ways they never had before. My being felt utterly open, utterly indistinguishable from the beings of what had until then seemed to be other separate humans.

The intensity of this experience has diminished as time has passed and as I have spent more time in the everyday world, although the perspective of empty, nondual, boundless

LIBERATING THE SELF

space has remained accessible to me whenever I want it. One month or so later, I have also continued to deal with an extraordinary volume of personal shadow material that comes up on a more or less daily basis. My capacity for repression seems to have weakened almost into nonexistence. While I think this is ultimately a positive aspect of Awakening, dealing with this level of baggage so consistently can be exhausting, and it has also led to the facing of certain truths about myself and my past actions that have been seriously unpleasant. Day by day I am becoming more and more authentic, which is both profoundly rewarding and extremely hard work. This has been at once the most transformative, the best, and the hardest experience of my life.

A crucial element of this experience for me was having some advance warning of what might happen. From reading and listening to accounts of the Awakenings of others, as well as from conversations with Mugen Sensei and my previous teachers, I knew that going to the limit of one's sanity and perhaps even a little beyond, as well as having unimaginably intense experiences of fear and other negative emotions, was not uncommon in this spiritual territory. Knowing, in the darkest moments, that what you're experiencing is somehow normal—this justifies having some faith and trust that you will come out the other side. This faith and trust can make all the difference. My hope is that this account may be helpful in this way for others.

—STUDENT 2

AUTHOR'S NOTE: Mu is generally the first *kōan* a student engages in *kōan* study. A young monk was walking with deeply realized Chan teacher Joshu. A dog wandered past them. The monk asked Joshu, "Does that dog have Buddha nature?" Although all of Buddhism agrees that all sentient beings have the nature to be fully realized Buddhas, Joshu said, "Mu." Mu means something like "not" or "without." This *kōan* has engaged students for over a thousand years.

PART II

Unwinding and Releasing

WHEN THE TIME COMES to more fully orient toward and invest in the unconditioned truth of the Absolute, it is challenging. We have put an immense level of energy and fastidious commitment into creating and maintaining this sense of self over many years. On a deep-knowing level, we are beginning to feel and witness the falseness, the fakeness, of this constructed self. We know from our time in dual unity with the Presence and love of the Absolute that we are part of something much larger; we know we are always held in and by love. Yet it can be hard to release the dysfunction we know so well for the uncertainty of an unstructured and unfettered abiding in the Absolute.

As the moment approaches when we need to release all that is false to fully embrace what is unconditioned and authentic, our mind panics. Questions arise as our fear grows. *What if I let my sense of self go and there is nothing to replace it? Will I lose my mind? If I get to my most mysterious depths in the Absolute, how will I function? How will I maintain relationships? How will I be able to maintain work performance? Can I survive without a self, a me?* These are common concerns that appear as we turn toward unconditioned truth.

As Part 1, "Revealing and Updating," has shown, within ourselves we will encounter many resistances to truth and clarity on the path of Awakening, and we may choose to invest more fully in the false narrative of a me or maintain a blurry or opaque perspective on our behaviors and feelings, rather than face a fear of failure—or success. For many reasons, we humans prefer to abide in uncertainty and vagueness, in fakeness.

> *Our thirst for truth, our blazing inner flame of truth, must burn so hot that we can only reach for the depths of understanding, regardless of what we will meet and confront with compassion.*

To leave this state of uncertainty or falseness, our thirst for truth, our blazing inner flame of truth, must burn so hot that we can only reach for the depths of understanding, regardless of what we will meet and confront with compassion. The reward of ultimate truth must finally supersede our need to contract and protect our personal dysfunction.

My own journey with truth and clarity has taken a complicated path. In my turn away from the union with the Presence of the Absolute, I, like all children, blamed myself. I felt the Absolute had rejected me for a fundamental flaw, a brokenness that was irreparable. My belief in this fundamental flaw led me to act with grandiose narcissistic bravado whenever I felt insignificant or invisible in my life.

This was a fiction I perpetuated to convince myself and all others I was not broken at my core. I lied constantly and consistently, to myself and others, about who I was and what my skills and abilities were. I tried to project exclusively my together, accomplished, stress-free self. (The made-up self!)

When first encountering truth, I was confounded. How do I invite truth into my inner world without disrupting the multilayered levels of me about which I had so thoroughly convinced myself?

With a deepening meditation and spiritual practice, I became more and more thoroughly committed to the truth. Not my truth but objective, verifiable, universal truth. Once my allegiance to truth was fully landed, it no longer mattered where I went in my interior, my psychological structuring. If orienting to the unconditioned truth meant I had to sacrifice my cherished layers of egoic structuring in my personality, I became willing to make that sacrifice. Truth tasted better to me than my habituated inner lies and patent falsehoods.

I was loosening my allegiance to the me through abiding and resting in unconditioned, universal truth.

Interestingly, the more I gravitated toward truth over maintaining my sense of self, the less attached I was to maintaining this artificial me. I was loosening my allegiance to the me through abiding and resting in unconditioned, universal truth. Truth became my pursuit and my prize. I was orienting toward truth and becoming more authentic myself as deeper and more sustained contact with the Absolute became my practice and reality.

This part of the book contains practices that will likewise help you loosen, unwind, and release your allegiance to the me. We begin with the *samatha* (purification-of-mind) practices called "Thirty-Two Body Parts," "Skeleton Meditation," and "*Kasinas*." As awareness and perception drop beneath conceptual knowing with each of these practices, our firm conviction that each aspect of our physicality and mentality is our ultimate reality loosens and lessens. When I did these practices, I unconsciously believed that once each of these parts of my body was removed, I would find a little black box labeled "me." Reality did not match my expectation. Instead, when I landed fully in the last characteristic or quality of each meditation, there was nothing remaining, just void Absence. There was no me.

In Chapter 4, the second section of Part II, we turn to protective meditations, specifically innate goodness meditation, foulness meditation, and death recollection. We practice these to ensure we have lots of inner stability before awareness and consciousness journey into other realms.

Practicing innate goodness as a protective meditation supports the softening of our inner negative talk and negative self-judgments. Innate goodness affords us an experience of inner buoyancy and optimistic uplift.

By engaging in foulness meditation, we diminish our allegiance and favoritism toward our particular body and self by leaning toward its unpleasant functions.

Death recollection loosens our thought-concept supporting this body and this life as primary identities by prompting us to hold squarely that this life is quite finite, and therefore we have no time to waste on deferring wholehearted engagement with spiritual practice and meditation.

Once we have identified and released our compulsive attachments to the body as a foundation of our identity, we turn to direct contact with the Absolute. Because we have loosened our self-definition, we will find identities such as our body or body boundary lessening and falling out of perception. This prepares awareness and consciousness to feel more comfort journeying away from the perception of the body in its location. We chiefly employ *shikantaza* meditation (just sitting) to quiet the identity assertions of the body/mind and open ourselves to traversing mysterious realms with breathtaking beauty. *Shikantaza* meditation is the focus of Chapter 5, the third section of Part II. Following each of these practices, I have included reflections on my personal experiences engaging with them.

CHAPTER 3

SAMATHA (PURIFICATION-OF-MIND) PRACTICES

IN TRADITIONAL THERAVADA BUDDHISM, a student is initially directed to the *samatha* portion of the path of practice. *Samatha* practices purify our allegiance to the sense of self through deep meditative concentration, and so they are also considered purification-of-mind practices.

Samatha translates as concentration, serenity, or tranquility. In effect, these meditations and practices experientially teach the student to focus on one meditative object at a time. This focus unifies awareness while balancing energy and meditative concentration.

Typically, the student new to Theravada Buddhism starts with breath awareness meditation, *ānāpānasati*. "*Ānāpāna*" is translated as breath and "*sati*" is translated as awareness. Breath awareness meditation is quite simple in its instruction: Breathe, and know you are breathing, right now, in the region between the nostrils and upper lip. Breath awareness meditation helps us to soften and quiet the mind as awareness naturally becomes more focused and as we loosen our mental grip on our customary sense of self. While the most succinct instruction contains all that is needed to undertake this meditation, personality distractions result in this being a meditation that takes time and perseverance to master. (For more details about breath awareness meditation, see the introduction to my book *Demystifying Awakening*.)

There are three levels of meditative concentration available in *samatha* practices:

1 Momentary concentration is simply when your awareness is in this moment, this breath. It is applying our awareness to the single meditative object in *samatha* concentration and meditation.

2 Access concentration commences when the meditator is able to maintain awareness on the meditative object for a *minimum* of fifteen to twenty minutes without serious interruption. A serious interruption occurs when awareness is firmly away from the meditative object. Should awareness maintain contact with the meditative object concurrently with a random thought, emotion, or memory, that is not a serious interruption.

In access concentration, we will also encounter the *jhāna* factors:

— Applied awareness (*vitakka*) is the intentional application of awareness to the solitary meditative object. Whenever we catch awareness drifting to another subject or object and we recognize the wandering, we return awareness to that single meditative object. Each time we realize we were distracted and return to the meditative object, we experience a slight purification of mind. We are electing our meditative object over mind wanderings and habits of personality.

— Sustained awareness (*vicāra*) maintains awareness on the single meditative object. When awareness is with our meditative object we want to relax our doing, ever so slightly lessening our intention of awareness. It is not that we wish to depart from the meditative object but rather that we want to invite the active participation of the Absolute in our meditation. Typically, when *vicāra* is actively present, we will feel a shift of activity. We gently lessen our personal effort, and when timely, we will feel a distinct deepening of the meditation. This is the appropriate response to *vicāra*. When we feel clearly with the meditative object, relax our effort without lessening our awareness on the meditative object, and awareness *departs* from the meditative object, that is a sign either that we lessened our effort too early or that we withdrew too much effort. This demonstrates the artistry of meditation. Often, we have to gauge where we are in our meditation practice and test to see the right amount of effort or relaxation needed to invite the Absolute to actively join the meditation.

— Joy (*pīti*) is a bodily felt enthusiasm. It's a bubbly physical sensation of ease. People report such good body feelings that they meditate for longer periods without discomfort or pain.

— Bliss (*sukha*) is the experience of everything being just right exactly as it is. It is an effervescent uplift of mental ease. *Sukha* soothes and calms mental activity that typically would distract the meditator.

— One-pointedness awareness (*ekaggatā*) is experienced as a continual, deliberate focusing of awareness. Awareness begins in meditation as a broad light illuminating the entire room. With access concentration, the ambient light illuminating the room narrows and focuses. It now appears more like a flashlight or torch clearly pointing to a distinct meditative object. As access concentration deepens to the third type of concentration, known as absorption or *jhāna*, the awareness has now focused further to a laser pointedness. This sharp laser focus of awareness guides the meditator deeper into the meditation to the point that all markers of a self become transparent, thoughts slow and stop, and our awareness merges into the specific meditative object.

3   Absorption or *jhāna* concentration is only available with *samatha* meditations. (Every meditation contains the first two levels of concentration.) It is the progressive sharpening and focusing of awareness to the degree it can penetrate all psychological structures of a self, slow or stop thoughts, and thoroughly, indivisibly merge with the meditative object while the *jhāna* concentration lasts. When the *jhāna* meditative energy begins to lessen, the absorption experience will dissolve, leaving the meditator resting in access concentration.

The eight breath awareness *jhānas* preceded the Buddha's day, and he practiced them throughout his life, beginning as a young ascetic. They have the distinction of being the final spiritual or meditative practice the Buddha engaged before dying. The *jhānas* (concentration absorption) are a no-self experience of a nondual state. The term "no-self" means there is no inner perception or self-referencing during the experience. There are awareness and consciousness but no inner sense of a me. A nondual state means that one's consciousness is within an undivided unity, a completeness with no remainders.

In First *Jhāna*, the first of the eight potential *jhānas*, awareness perceives nondual reality as a kind of energy or sound frequency. Over sustained practice and repeated trips into First *Jhāna*, our consciousness and awareness begin to slowly match the highest sound frequency of First *Jhāna*. When we match the highest frequency of First *Jhāna*, we can then orient toward Second *Jhāna*. This process of raising the sound frequency of our consciousness and awareness continues through each breath awareness *jhāna* up to and including the highest or Eighth *Jhāna*.

As we raise the sound frequency of our awareness and consciousness, we receive and enjoy a more purified mind with significantly less attachment to our customary sense of self. This affords us a temporary freedom from the oppression of the usual sense of self.

I knew almost nothing about *jhāna* practice when I attended a two-month retreat in 2005 with the Venerable Pa Auk Sayadaw. Reputed to be one of the great *jhāna* masters, a gifted meditator, and a well-respected Buddhist scholar, the Sayadaw had a book available online for free called *Knowing and Seeing*, but I found it too dense to read except when I was practicing a particular section of material. Besides this book, there was little information about *jhāna* practice available in English at that time.

I entered the retreat with few expectations simply because I did not know what the practice entailed. However, I found the first instruction quite clear—to be with the breath in the *ānāpāna* region (between the nostrils and upper lip). Furthermore, staying close to the breath on and off the cushion was fairly comfortable for me as I had learned to hold a *kōan* closely in prior practice. (A *kōan* is a spiritual paradox that cannot be resolved through the application of the conceptual mind. Our thoughts and prior history will not be of any assistance. We hold the *kōan* close at first like a repeated mantra. In time it lands well in awareness. We then can keep the *kōan* close—on the tip of our breath.) During our interview on the first or second day of the retreat, I startled the Sayadaw with my response to his question of how long I could stay with the breath. I said, "The better question is 'How long am I not with the breath?'" My answer to this was "a few minutes each day." Hearing my response, the Sayadaw flashed a beaming smile.

In that retreat, I meditated between fifteen and twenty-four hours each day. As the eight *jhānas* began to arise, I was startled at the deep, potent, powerful energy of the quality of the absorption and at the deep purification of mind and loosening of identity that was a benefit of each of the eight *jhānas*. The Sayadaw required me to spend three hours, uninterrupted, in each *jhāna* before I could receive the instructions for the next *jhāna*. He also required me to enter and exit each *jhāna* at will in his presence. I suspect he was checking my inner state to ensure it was full *jhāna* rather than access concentration, the level of concentration that precedes *jhāna* absorption.

Each of the first four *jhānas* feels to be located in the body. The purification they bring to mind and body feels quite intimate and increasingly potent. I was often left feeling blown out, expanded beyond what was remotely familiar. The Fifth through Eighth *Jhānas* feel to be outside the body in other realms. With each, there is a distinct experience of awareness and consciousness journeying through the top of the head (the crown chakra) into the particular realm (formless *jhāna*).

After completing the three-hour requirement for each *jhāna*, I also discovered that it was possible to access the Ninth *Jhāna*—the Absolute realm—from access concentration of the Eighth *Jhāna*. That led to me setting a resolution to enter and abide in the Absolute—entering Cessation, *Nibbāna* itself—for three hours without interruption. Today I would never recommend that a student set such a long time resolve for a first experience of the Absolute. Spending three hours in Cessation in my first journey was as profound and overwhelming as you might imagine. It took me about eighteen months to fully integrate the effects and changes I sustained during that powerful retreat with the Sayadaw.

After that retreat, the Sayadaw asked me to write a book on the practice for other Westerners. I wrote a first draft and then convinced another student who had also completed the *samatha* path on that retreat to be my coauthor. Shortly thereafter, I was informed that the Sayadaw had authorized me to teach the *samatha* practices, recognizing me as a *jhāna* master due to the depth of my practice on the retreat.

In jhāna practice, we begin to see who we might be and how we might function without the ever-present self.

The *jhāna* practice is an amazing, mind-blowing, life-altering practice. I can, and could, see the importance of this practice particularly when it is done to the depth of no thought and no sense of me. We begin to see who we might be and how we might function without the ever-present self.

Once a practitioner completes the progression of the eight breath awareness *jhānas* under a qualified *jhāna* master, the meditative practice can move on with additional concentration meditation practices, such as those we will explore next: "Thirty-Two Body Parts," "Skeleton Meditation," and *"Kasinas."*

Thirty-Two Body Parts

Thirty-two body parts is a reductive meditation. Through the practice, we clearly identify and establish a felt sense of each body part beneath the concept of that body part. The process of intentionally being with a body part causes it to peel itself away from the sense of self.

The first twenty of the thirty-two body parts are grouped in four sets of five parts. These are chiefly solidly physical and are seen predominantly as expressions of the earth element.

SET ONE:

1 Head hairs
2 Body hairs
3 Nails
4 Teeth
5 Skin

SET TWO:

6 Flesh
7 Sinews
8 Bones
9 Bone marrow
10 Kidneys

SET THREE:

11 Heart
12 Liver
13 Membrane
14 Spleen
15 Lungs

SET FOUR:

16 Intestines
17 Mesentery
18 Gorge
19 Feces
20 Brain

The twelve remaining body parts are grouped in two sets of six parts. These are chiefly solidly liquid and are seen predominantly as expressions of the water element.

SET FIVE:

21 Bile
22 Phlegm
23 Pus
24 Blood
25 Sweat
26 Fat

SET SIX:

27 Tears
28 Grease
29 Saliva
30 Snot
31 Synovia
32 Urine

Thirty-Two-Body-Parts Meditation Practice

I recommend getting a picture or other aid to locate the different body parts before you get started. Look up each part now to see exactly where it is and what it does in the body. Refer to this picture as needed while you work with each body part.

- Begin with the first body part: head hairs.
- Start by looking in a mirror at your head hairs.
- When you feel you have a clear mental picture of head hairs, close your eyes and check whether you can clearly see head hairs with eyes closed. Note for those who are not visual meditators: Seeing the head hairs with eyes closed may be too challenging. Try deeply feeling into head hairs.
- When your awareness settles beneath the concept, the mental knowing, of head hairs, how do head hairs feel to you? Stay with the felt sense of head hairs or the visual of head hairs for visual meditators. Let awareness drop below the conceptual or mental knowing to contact direct, nonconceptual knowing.

- Rest awareness in the nonconceptual knowing of head hairs. When you feel you know head hairs in a direct, nonconceptual knowing, shift to the second part of the first set, body hairs.
- Go through each part slowly until you can get meditatively deep enough to hold Set One as a unit and distinctly feel each part of Set One specifically and concretely.
- Once you deeply know the parts of the first set on a direct, nonconceptual basis, start the same process with the parts of Set Two.
- Once you arrive at a place where you can feel the deep, nonconceptual quality of each part of Set Two, return to the first set and run through each part to that same level or depth. Then do Set One and then Set Two as a unit.
- Continue with each set as outlined above until you can hold all six sets as discrete units while also distinctly feeling each part of each set.

In reaching the conclusion of this practice, we can have a visceral knowing that identifying and thereby removing each body part ends in nothing. There are no remainders after subtracting each body part. This means that once all body parts are recognized and released, there is no discernible me.

My Experience with Thirty-Two-Body-Parts Meditation

My experience with this practice was mixed at first. I understood this was a foundational Theravada meditation practice but could not immediately witness its possible benefits. Furthermore, I had to research the function of many of these body parts and where in the body they were located.

It was interesting to me that I would have memories or perspectives on a variety of body parts. If, for example, I had been injured in a particular body part, I often found the memory and the emotions associated with that memory in the field of that body part. Because there had been an injury, I had an emotional connection to that body part in direct relationship to the mental suffering I experienced at that time. Any assumptions or beliefs I held had to be examined thoroughly to see if they were true.

As the practice progressed, I could see that staying with the felt sense of each body part allowed me to resolve any beliefs or issues I had with that body part, and consequently that body part dropped out of my definition of me.

Advanced Practice

After deeply practicing the thirty-two body parts
in your own body, you can attempt to discern
these same body parts in another person. Typically,
you would select someone to whom you are not
romantically attracted.

- Follow the same order of body parts—begin with
  head hairs. Hold the visual of the other person's
  head hairs until you can either see or have a felt
  sense of them with eyes closed.
- Stay with the other's head hairs until you drop
  beneath the conceptual knowing to direct, intuitive, nonconceptual knowing. Once you deeply
  know the other's head hairs, shift to the second
  part, body hairs, and practice as instructed above.
- Continue to work through the other person's
  body parts, following all the steps you took for
  your parts.

Skeleton Meditation

After meditating with each nonconceptual body part of the thirty-two body parts, we turn our awareness toward a core identity: the structure of the body itself.

To develop and practice skeleton meditation, we start by first turning our awareness to one of the thirty-two body parts—bones.

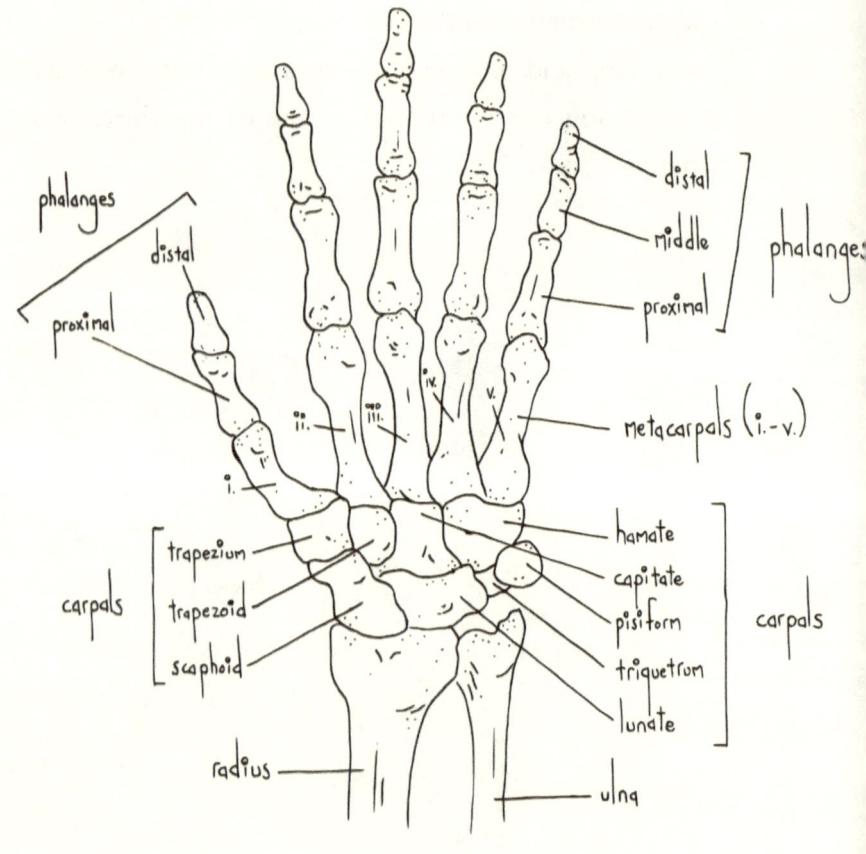

phalanges

distal

proximal

distal

middle

proximal

phalanges

proximal

ii.

iii.

iv.

v.

i.

metacarpals (i.-v.)

trapezium

trapezoid

scaphoid

carpals

hamate

capitate

pisiform

triquetrum

lunate

carpals

radius

ulna

Skeleton Meditation Practice

- For the visual mediator: Start by picturing a bone, any bone. When you can meditate upon a bone with eyes closed, stay with the direct experience of bone until you feel awareness drop beneath the conceptual knowing to direct, intuitive, nonconceptual knowing.
- For the felt-sense meditator: Feel into one of your bones. Stay with the felt sense until you can feel it beneath the conceptual knowing. Rest in the direct, intuitive, nonconceptual knowing of bone.
- For visual and felt-sense meditators: Stay with the initial bone until awareness drops beneath the concept of bone. Then observe awareness expand to a cojoined bone. Develop concentration on the nonconceptual level. Allow awareness to continue expanding to cojoined bones until you can perceive your entire skeleton.

Once we have experienced our body as its specific parts, the concept of the physical sense of self is weakened and reduced.

My Experience with Skeleton Meditation

At first the idea of this practice was unappealing to me. It seemed like busy work to my impatient mind. Yet as I undertook this practice, I was riveted by the reality that I was actually seeing my skeleton. I could see discoloration in the bones, places that were chipped or had been broken and healed. As with the thirty-two-body-parts meditation, I was able to identify the surface layer of self-definition—the conceptual identity of each part—of the skeleton. I also had to process my gratitude for this skeleton. It had protected me during various life events when I was injured.

Being with the parts and the whole of the skeleton allowed awareness to drop beneath the concept of skeleton and be with the direct, nonverbal felt sense. I was releasing the concept of me as skeleton. Prior to this meditation practice, I was my body. It was a primary, preverbal identity. I had formed the perspective that this body is me before I had language. Engaging this practice allowed me to loosen the grip identity held on the body and the body boundary, that is, the conviction that the me ends at the edge of the skin.

When I began the advanced practice, I was riveted. I recall being in the retreat's main dining room, looking around, and watching a roomful of skeletons eating and drinking. This experience also permitted me to stop seeing another's body as an expression of their sense of self.

Advanced Practice

- When you are at the point of being with your entire skeleton beneath the conceptual level of knowing in direct, nonconceptual knowing, select another person whose skeleton you will practice seeing. Choose someone for whom you do not feel any romantic attraction.
- Take one of their fingers as your beginning meditative object. Let awareness drop beneath the surface of conceptual knowing to the direct, intuitive, nonconceptual knowing of the other's finger bone. Stay with the perception of their bone until you are sensing or seeing it clearly.
- Expand your awareness to take in the next bone on their hand.
- Repeat the process until you can hold their entire skeleton in your awareness as direct, intuitive, nonconceptual knowing.

Kasinas

Next, we turn our meditation practice toward removing the conceptual attachment we have to colors and related parts of the body. We do this through meditative practice with *kasinas*. *Kasinas* are mind-made, disklike objects that can be perceived meditatively by either visual or felt-sense contact. There are color *kasinas*, four element *kasinas* (earth, water, fire, and air), and two very subtle *kasinas*, light *kasina* and space *kasina*.

Color Kasinas

With each of the color *kasinas*, we are working with a color that is found in the body: white, brown or black, yellow, and red. Meditating with the color *kasinas* helps us disidentify with that color and with whatever meaning or identity we have for it. For example, perhaps we have a beautiful head of hair. In some respects, we feel, *I am my hair*. If we work the color of our hair as a color *kasina*, we will release some of the belief in our body-as-me identity. This lessens our allegiance to the body as identity and self while letting us open more to the potential of deep Awakening—Awakening of the Absolute to itself in our location.

White *Kasina*

- Begin by reestablishing skeleton meditation. Meditatively contact your skeleton at the level of direct, intuitive, nonconceptual knowing. Spend one meditation period resting in nonconceptual knowing of your skeleton.
- In your next meditation, spend fifteen minutes resting in direct, nonconceptual knowing of your skeleton.
- Now shift your awareness to directly perceive the rounded white portion of the back of your skull. Narrow awareness to hold exclusively that portion of the back of your skull.
- Holding awareness to that round, white portion of your skull, let all else about your skeleton drop away.
- With steady awareness on the whiteness of the back of your skull, let the rounded whiteness be your meditative object.
- Stay with the round whiteness of your skull. Maintain awareness here until you drop beneath the conceptual knowing of your skull. Sense into the direct, intuitive, nonconceptual awareness of rounded whiteness.

- With sustained meditative practice on the rounded whiteness, we can develop or progress from momentary concentration to access concentration.
- In access concentration, we can stay with the rounded whiteness with increasing stability and clarity. This rounded whiteness can begin to feel energized and present as stunningly bright white.
- Allow the whiteness to continue expanding as it wishes. Do not rush expanding the whiteness. Take it slow, permitting the expanding white *nimitta* to stay solid and substantially whole. (A *nimitta* is a mind-made product, a sign, of deep concentration meditation on an unchanging meditative object.)
- The expanded whiteness can develop into full absorption concentration, the final level of concentration meditation also called *jhāna*.

Whether the white *kasina* develops into *jhāna* or deep access concentration is not of vital importance. What is important is an allowing, a surrendering, to the bright whiteness while the meditator connects deeply with the direct, intuitive, nonconceptual knowing of whiteness.

We are preparing ourselves to potentially open to the Absolute's pure, wholesome love.

Being deeply with the whiteness of white *kasina* relaxes any reluctance or hesitation we will encounter when approaching the bright white quality of unconditioned universal love in the manifest Absolute. We are preparing ourselves to potentially open to the Absolute's pure, wholesome love.

Brown or Black *Kasina*

For this *kasina*, we are using our head or body hairs as a starting point. Those with non-brunette head and body hair should select someone with dark, shiny hair for this *kasina* practice.

- Stare at one or more of your head or body hairs, letting awareness drop beneath any meaning or history you have with your hair or body hair color to the deep, intuitive, nonconceptual knowing of that color. How does that color feel to you intuitively?
- Compare the color to the whiteness of white *kasina*. Do these feel different or the same? If different, how are they different, specifically? If they feel to have a lot of sameness, how are they similar or related? Where are these two colors not the same?
- As you clearly identify in your own experience how hair or body hair color is different, in its felt sense, from white *kasina*, dive deeply into the head or body hair color. Feel the color directly without any thoughts, ideas, or history.
- Notice where in your world this head or body hair color is seen. On other heads? In advertisements? Where?

By noticing where this color occurs on our body and externally, we loosen the identity we have with this color. We see it is a color appearing in many aspects of life. It is not just our color. It is everyone else's color, too.

Yellow *Kasina*

As we feel a lessening of our attachment to and identity with head or body hair color, we can move on to the yellow *kasina*. For yellow *kasina*, either we can return to the thirty-two-body-parts meditation and focus on our urine in our bladder, or we can focus on yellow flowers or yellow leaves on trees.

- Whatever your initial contact is with the color yellow, gaze at the yellow until it seems to deeply land in your awareness. Visual meditators, you should be clearly seeing the brightness of the color yellow when you close your eyes.
- For felt-sense meditators: Gaze at the color yellow until it feels to be landed internally in your awareness. When you close your eyes, do you feel the color yellow as clearly and as vibrantly as you did with eyes open?
- Stay with the visual or felt sense of yellow. You may feel memories and thought-concepts related to yellow softening and beginning to fall or drop away. That is expected.
- Maintain awareness on the perception of yellow until you feel a shift to a more neutral relationship to yellow.

Red *Kasina*

For the color red, we can return to the thirty-two-body-parts meditation to connect with the blood, or we can use red flowers or leaves on trees as our meditative object.

— Whatever your initial contact is with the color red, gaze at the red until it seems to land in your awareness. Visual meditators, when you close your eyes, you should be clearly seeing the vividness of the color red.
— For felt-sense meditators: Gaze at the color red until it feels to be landed internally in your awareness. When you close your eyes, do you feel the color red as clearly and vibrantly as you did with eyes open?
— Stay with the visual or felt sense of the color red. You may feel memories and thought identity related to red softening and beginning to fall or drop away. That is expected.
— Maintain awareness on the perception of red until you feel a shift to a more neutral relationship to red.

Four Element Kasinas

The four elements that make up all of physical reality are earth, water, fire, and air. Here we explore how to practice each element as a *kasina*. Following the four element *kasinas*, we will also explore light *kasina* and space *kasina*.

Earth *Kasina*

We can develop earth *kasina* in a couple of ways.

- Go outside and find a patch of bare earth. It should be free of any growth, rocks, or debris.
- Using a stick, draw a circle within the patch of bare earth.
- Alternatively, you can fill a jar or pot with clean dirt with no growth or debris in it.
- Sitting near this patch of earth, view the circle intently. (Or do the same with the contents of the jar.) Really let yourself become intimate with earth. Drop beneath the conceptual knowing of earth to the deeper, nonconceptual felt sense of what earth feels like internally, intuitively.
- Let yourself feel your connection to earth, how you have earthlike qualities in your being. When humans die, their bodies begin to decay. Eventually much of this once-robust body is returned to earth, to dirt.
- Feel the softening of your beliefs in your own physical solidity. Allow the memories of your strong, solid physicality to relax to match your felt sense of nonconceptual earth—earth as something known in deep intuition rather than through memories and history.

- Let this mental picture of earth or the felt sense of the circle of earth become your sole meditative object. Invite the softening of your attachment to ideas about or prior experiences with the solidity of yourself or your world.
- Off the cushion, look around at all you see. What belief or story do you carry about earth? Is it a level or reality that cannot be questioned? Is it timeless?

Water *Kasina*

When working with earth *kasina* results in a sizable shift in your relationship to earth and all solid phenomena, turn toward water *kasina*. We can develop water *kasina* in a couple of ways.

- Go outside and find a pool or pond with standing water. Identify a small section of that pool or pond of water. It should be free of any growth, rocks, or debris.
- Alternatively, you can fill a cup, glass, or jar with water to use indoors.
- Sitting near the water source, view the water intently. Really let yourself become intimate with water. Drop beneath the conceptual knowing of water to the deeper, nonconceptual felt sense of what water feels like internally, intuitively. Feel how the flow aspect of water impacts you. Can you feel flow in your consciousness? What exactly does that feel like?
- Let yourself feel your connection to water, how you have water-like qualities in your being.
- Feel the softening of your beliefs in your own physical solidity and flow. Allow the memories of your strong, solid physicality to relax to match your felt sense of nonconceptual water—water as

something known in deep intuition rather than through memories and history.

- Let this mental picture or the felt sense of water become your sole meditative object. Invite the softening of your attachment to ideas about or prior experiences with the solidity of yourself or your world.
- Off the cushion, look around at all the locations of water you see. What belief or story do you carry about water? Is it a level or reality that cannot be questioned? Is it timeless?

Fire *Kasina*

When working with water *kasina* results in a sizable shift in your relationship to water and all flowing or liquid phenomena, turn toward fire *kasina*. We can develop fire *kasina* in a couple of ways.

- Light a candle or build a safe fire in a firepit or fireplace.
- Sitting near the fire source, view the fire intently. Really let your awareness become intimate with fire. Drop beneath the conceptual knowing of fire to the deeper, nonconceptual felt sense of what fire feels like internally, intuitively. Feel how the flickering aspect of fire impacts you. Can you feel flickering in your consciousness? What exactly does that feel like? How is it different than earth or water in its felt sense?
- Let yourself feel your connection to fire, how you have hot, warm, flickering, fire-like qualities— including the destructive quality and function of fire—in your being.
- Feel the softening of your beliefs in your own physical solidity, heat, and physical and emotional warmth. Allow the memories of your strong, solid physicality to relax to match your felt sense of nonconceptual fire—fire as

something known in deep intuition rather than
through memories and history.

— Let this mental picture or the felt sense of fire
become your sole meditative object. Invite the
softening of your attachment to ideas about or
prior experiences with the solidity of yourself
or your world.

— Off the cushion, look around at all the locations
of fire you see. What belief or story do you carry
about fire? Is it a level or reality that cannot be
questioned? Is it timeless?

Air *Kasina*

When working with fire *kasina* results in a sizable shift in your relationship to fire and all warm or hot phenomena within, turn to air *kasina*. We can develop air *kasina* in a couple of ways.

- Go to a door or window that opens to the outside. Feel and watch the air entering and exiting. See how the air moves curtains or notice other observable phenomena.
- Alternatively, go outside and watch the air gently move the tree branches or leaves. See how the flowers and grasses sway when touched by air.
- Sitting where you can perceive the expression and function of air, view the air intently. Really let your awareness become intimate with air. Drop beneath the conceptual knowing of air to the deeper, nonconceptual felt sense of what air feels like internally, intuitively. Feel how the flowing aspect of air impacts you. Can you feel flowing in your consciousness? What exactly does that feel like? How is it different than earth, water, or fire in its felt sense?
- Let yourself feel your connection to air, how in your being you have air-like qualities of flowing and obstructions to flow. You may even feel the

destructive quality and function of air. Large
storms and hurricanes have fast-moving air that
can destroy houses and other solid buildings or
structures.

— Feel the softening of your beliefs in your own
physical solidity, in air, and in physical and emotional flow. Allow the memories of your strong,
solid physicality to relax to match your felt sense
of nonconceptual air—air as something known
in deep intuition rather than through memories
and history.

— Let this mental picture or the felt sense of air
become your sole meditative object. Invite the
softening of your attachment to ideas about or
prior experiences with the solidity of yourself or
your world.

— Off the cushion, look around at all the locations
of air you see. What belief or story do you carry
about air or flow? Is it a level or reality that
cannot be questioned? Is it timeless?

Light *Kasina*

When working with air *kasina* results in a sizable shift in your relationship to air and flow phenomena within, turn to light *kasina*. We can develop light *kasina* in a couple of ways.

- Go to a door or window that opens to the outside. Feel and watch the rays of light streaming into the room.
- Alternatively, go outside and watch the rays of light move gently through the tree branches or leaves. See how the flowers and grasses change coloring based upon how and when they are touched by light.
- Sitting where you can perceive the expression and function of light, view the light intently. Really let your awareness become intimate with light. Drop beneath the conceptual knowing of light to the deeper, nonconceptual felt sense of what light feels like internally, intuitively. Feel how the radiant aspect of light impacts you. Can you feel radiance in your consciousness? What exactly does that feel like? How is it different than earth, water, fire, or air in its felt sense?
- Let yourself feel your connection to light, how in your being you have light-like qualities

of radiance and obstructions to radiance. As humans die, their bodies begin to decay and lose their radiance.

— Feel the softening of your beliefs in your own physical solidity, light, and radiance, and notice how they invite greater inner tenderness. Allow the memories of your strong, solid physicality to relax to match your felt sense of nonconceptual light—light as something known in deep intuition rather than through memories and history.

— Let this mental picture or felt sense of light become your sole meditative object. Invite the softening of your attachment to ideas about or prior experiences with the solidity of yourself or your world.

— Off the cushion, look around at all the examples of light you see. What belief or story do you carry about light and radiance? Is it a level or reality that cannot be questioned? Is it timeless?

Space *Kasina*

When working with light *kasina* results in a sizable shift in your relationship to light and radiance phenomena within, explore space *kasina*. We can develop space *kasina* in a couple of ways.

- Go to a door or window that opens to the outside. Observe the openness of the window or door. Can you detect where the door or window is not? That is one form of space.
- Alternatively, go outside, lie down, and watch the sky where there are no clouds or other phenomena. Let awareness drift toward that open space of sky. Allow awareness to expand into that openness of space. View the space intently.
- Really let your awareness become intimate with space. Drop beneath the conceptual knowing of space to the deeper, nonconceptual felt sense of what space feels like internally, intuitively. Feel how the openness aspect of space impacts you. Can you feel unstructured openness in your consciousness? What exactly does that feel like? How is it different than earth, water, fire, air, or light in its felt sense? Space is the canvas upon which all form is expressed. Let that reality sink in and land in your consciousness.

- Let yourself feel your connection to space, how you have space-like qualities in your experience of your body.
- Feel the softening of your beliefs in your own physical solidity, in space, and in physical and emotional flow. Allow the memories of your strong, solid physicality to relax to match your felt sense of nonconceptual space—space as something known in deep intuition rather than through memories and history.
- Let this mental picture or felt sense of space become your sole meditative object. Invite the softening of your attachment to ideas about or prior experiences with the solidity of yourself or your world.
- Off the cushion, look around at all the locations of space you witness. What belief or story do you carry about space? Is it a level or reality that cannot be questioned? Is it timeless?

My Experience with Kasinas

At the start, I found that working with *kasinas* was challenging. They are mind-made objects. Typically, we find a quality, such as space, in the world. We fixate on that quality until, with eyes closed, there is a visual or felt-sense clarity of the object. Somehow, we know what space looks like whether it is a quality of the sky or something observed when looking through the holes in a window screen.

As we start to discover how to work with the mental image, we are also dramatically deepening meditative concentration. The *kasinas* are used to open to *jhāna* (absorption). *Jhāna* with a *kasina* purifies our conceptual labeling and mental knowing of that quality. In *jhāna*, we recognize and release the conceptual definition as well as our conceptual history and experience with a particular quality of reality. This process loosens our grip on the me as identity. As we let go of what we take to be most real in our world and life, we are accessing greater freedom and purifying our mind.

CHAPTER 4

PROTECTIVE MEDITATIONS

NOW THAT WE HAVE penetrated the thirty-two-body-parts meditation, skeleton meditation, and *kasina* meditations to a nonconceptual level, we have directly experienced the body through its parts and pieces. While seeing these parts of the me concurrently, a disidentification occurs. Experiencing these parts of the me so clearly also liberates, frees, our self-definition, leaving an open spaciousness in its place. During this process, we have not discovered a particular source supporting the sense of self. We will continue our journey into the *samatha* practices by engaging what in Theravada Buddhism are called the protective meditations, which will ensure we have lots of inner stability before awareness and consciousness journey into other realms.

Our sense of self will be increasingly seen as an artifice, a psychological structure meant to imitate the free flow of love and the deep wisdom of the source—the Absolute.

The protective meditations offer us a shelter, a refuge, as we explore new territories, realms, and universes. Because we are opening to the natural fluidity of the worlds we mentally construct, our worldview can be deeply shaken. Our sense of self will be increasingly seen as an artifice, a psychological structure meant to imitate the free flow of love and the deep wisdom of the source—the Absolute.

Innate Goodness Meditation

One of the protective meditations is innate goodness, which helps us by keeping us connected to universal, unconditioned love.

Typically, we feel seen in our goodness only when we perform well for a caregiver, teacher, partner, or employer. We function in a way they appreciate, and they, in turn, relay that we did a good job. While we feel elated, we also know on a deeper level that we are being rewarded solely for our function, our performance, rather than for who we feel we are in our private moments. The validation therefore falls flat.

Innate goodness is the goodness of the source of all creation and manifestation—the Absolute. It has goodness and purity that touch us through uplifting buoyant qualities of the Absolute. It feels upbeat in its enthusiasm for rightness and truth. In practicing innate goodness meditation, we rest in the deep love and acceptance of the Absolute. We feel valued and seen in a thorough way.

The teaching on practicing this meditation can be found in Chapter 1.

Common Resistances to Innate Goodness

There are several common resistances to innate goodness, including a conviction in a core identity of being bad, a belief that we are too broken or damaged to be worthy of innate goodness, and a feeling at our core that we are worthless and/or unlovable.

— Conviction in a core identity of being bad: In our turn away from the source, we blame ourselves for being so damaged that the Absolute was justified in rejecting us, in throwing us out of the perfect union with Absolute love and Presence. Over time, our core wound becomes layered with avoidant strategies and failed attempts to meet the wound itself. In effect, its legend grows in our mind. The core wound feels to be worse than we imagined, we tell ourselves. Due to this avoidance and the strong belief in the truth of our core wound, we remove ourselves from the possibility of meeting and partaking of the Absolute's innate goodness.

— The belief that we are too broken or damaged to be worthy of innate goodness: This belief pattern, to expect the worst in most situations, is a protection. Should we expect the worst, we may be pleasantly surprised when it is just short of the worst anticipated result. When we couple this belief pattern with a confirmed sense of valuelessness, we become convinced that the Absolute will never be available to us. There is no point in even trying to meet the Absolute, let alone in opening to it and fully receiving it.

— A feeling at our core that we are worthless and/or unlovable: When we hold a self-belief that we are worthless or unlovable, we see ourselves as a rocky, barren field where no seeds of love will ever land, root, or grow. It is a sad truth we hold dear. We believe our core is so impoverished that there is no justifiable reason to even try to introduce love and acceptance.

My Experience with Innate Goodness Meditation

In my earlier days of Zen practice, I identified as a head-and-belly practitioner—"head" referring to understanding and knowing and "belly" referring to being grounded, seated in nonconceptual knowing. I had defensively turned down my heart contact. I was, however, fully able to love my partner, children, family, and friends. When I would demonstrate love toward myself or others I did not know well, it was extremely difficult. Further, I was very yoked to my stories of a deficient me, particularly my core wounding.

Over the past twenty years, I have been able to work more directly on my core wounding through closely tracking my life reactivity. When I observe myself acting disproportionately to a particular situation, I note it in my spiritual journal. Later, in a quiet, safe space, I refer back to the incident and, ultimately, undoubtedly discover an emotional nick to my core wound.

When I oriented to the pure love of the Absolute, I found a lightness, a buoyancy, that was revolutionary to me. I felt light and filled with love. The pure loving lightness I call "innate goodness" calmed and quieted the historic negative self-talk, affording me a vastness, an open, light space within. With this quality of Absolute love, I was able to move directly into the core wound—for me, a complete conviction that I was so broken, so damaged, that my own parents were unable to love me. And here I was basking in complete, perfect, objective love. Every part of me, every self-definition and belief, was loved fully and equally.

My orientation and dedication to truth became more important than protecting my core wound.

This experience with innate goodness supported my questioning of my belief in my core wound. I was able to more fully enter this bedrock self-belief with more objective curiosity. My orientation and dedication to truth became more important than protecting my core wound.

Foulness Meditation

The next meditation we undertake to continue loosening the sense of self is foulness meditation. Foulness meditation is intended to break down our conceptual allegiance to and reverence for our body based on our attractiveness and our handsome or beautiful qualities. We do this by leaning toward the unpleasant functions of this body.

Foulness Meditation Practice

- Settle yourself in a quiet position. Start with some deep-belly breaths, deeply relaxing into your meditation seat.
- With eyes closed, recall a corpse you have seen. In the event you have not personally seen a corpse, search for a picture of a decomposing corpse. We are searching for an image that conjures up a repulsed reaction in us.
- Let awareness drop beneath the thought-concept of a corpse or beneath a repulsed reaction to the corpse.
- Feel the space or spaciousness as awareness separates from the thought-concept of a repulsive corpse.
- Notice the deeply felt spaciousness resting in the tenderness of being loosely in union with your body.

There is a quality of freedom as we lessen our deep commitment to this body. Who are we if we are not just this particular body?

My Experience with Foulness Meditation

Foulness meditation was challenging for me at first. To engage this practice, I had to actively develop an orientation of repulsion toward the world, something that felt out of character. To explain what I mean, I need to provide some context about the Buddhist defilements, which are (1) desire or greed, (2) aversion or ill will, and (3) delusion. It is understood that while everyone has all three of these defilements, we each have an inherent proclivity for being predominantly either a desire or an aversion type. I am wired as a desire type. I was not committed to viewing life as something to be avoided or rejected. This made this practice more difficult for me than it might be for someone who is an aversion type. I have known a few aversion-type people who held the goal of Theravada Buddhism to be "getting off the wheel of existence." In other words, they anxiously await the final release, their death, to free them from the bonds of human life and human suffering.

Developing a tone of repulsion toward the world started with me reviewing the world and focusing exclusively on all that was wrong, broken, or damaged. Seeing just the ugliness of the world assisted me in landing in a viewpoint of repulsion toward the world, which, in turn, loosened my desire/greed grip on my life. Before this, I had unknowingly created an overly optimistic viewpoint. I had become an advocate for collecting pleasant experiences and subtly,

unconsciously, rejecting whatever was unwanted or unde-
sired. I discovered that my overly optimistic viewpoint was
just as false as fully engaging the aversion-type defilement
pattern. This practice assisted me in liberating some unconscious patterns and beliefs.

Dealth Recollection

Death recollection is a very potent and powerful practice. This is not an abstract, conceptual reflection on the concept of death. This is practicing and meditating to connect with and feel the witnessing of your body's demise. It is shockingly impactful to go through the process of death meditatively. On some level it feels quite real. It is intended to help us viscerally feel both that death is a reality for this physical structure and that we do not have unlimited time to practice and attend retreats.

Death Recollection Practice

- Start by returning to the foulness meditation practice. Maintain awareness on the image of the repulsive corpse. Hold that image until awareness settles beneath the thought-concepts of foulness and of the repulsiveness of the corpse.
- Let the foulness felt sense settle into your body image as your self-identity. In other words, be the repulsive corpse in your meditation.
- As your self-identity concepts soften and fall away, open awareness to the end of your life. The end of this very lifetime.
- Feel your body in its last hours or moments. Consider the most important attainments of this life. Notice if you feel a slight sense of loss that you did not engage with your spiritual and meditative practice more thoroughly and deeply. Let yourself commit genuinely and profoundly to your intention for further deepening spiritual and meditative practice.

My Experience with Death Recollection

As a child, I was fascinated by death. What was life? How did life go away in death? Where, if anywhere, did people go after death?

When the time came for this meditation, I was very excited to give it a try. Meditatively feeling and sensing the experience of the body winding down and approaching death was quite interesting. I could feel body systems shutting down. Awareness of the world around me slowly narrowed like a camera lens focusing on a very specific spot for a picture. My work identity, relationships, and history slowly fell away. Memories of my life also quieted and dropped off. I could feel the body organs quieting and ceasing their important life-giving functions. As my body felt like it was dying, I could see what I had done in my life that was worthy of reflection. I could also relax my grip on all my mistakes and errors, seeing I was not wrong in making them but simply human.

Tracking the felt experience of this body dying led to experiencing union with the Absolute. Whatever did not die was reabsorbed into the Absolute. I was merged again with the Absence, the peace, the love, and the Presence of the Absolute. I was able to return to my true home. I was welcome.

CHAPTER 5

SHIKANTAZA (SILENT ILLUMINATION MEDITATION)

AS OUR SPIRITUAL JOURNEY and meditation practice unfold, we move from seeing the world in duality of me and all else to a world of unity or Oneness.

The average person views their life and the world as a duality—a twoness. *I am this independent being over here, and you are another being over there. We are not connected to each other.* Because each of us views our self as a silo—a separate, independent being—we feel disconnected, adrift even, from the balance of life.

Duality also reveals our separation from objects we need or desire. Again, if I am this entirely independent being and what I want to feel good and happy in my life is that object over there, there is a twoness. I feel separate from what I want. This means I need to strategize to get that food or shelter or another want. I cannot trust any level of benevolence of the Absolute to ensure I will have my basic needs met. *My needs are met only through my individual efforts,* or so many of us believe.

There is a wonderful Zen expression of true reality: "not two, not one." This means that the concept, the idea, the belief in duality is a position of the mind. It is not real. Through sustained spiritual practice, the divisions or barriers of separation soften and drop. When the divisions of separation fall away, we are in contact with what feels like a unity, a Oneness.

With further spiritual work, we can realize that even the Oneness is a concept, an idea we project on the reality of the Absolute. When we fully grok, or fully get, that Oneness and unity are concepts, too, we can release those and be fully in a world of "not two, not one." It is just this. Just this moment. Just this direct experience of reality. This realization of "not two, not one" is called suchness or thusness in Buddhism.

One of the meditative methods we can use to contact "not two, not one"—thusness—is through *shikantaza* (from the Zen tradition).

Shikantaza, which is also known as silent illumination meditation, is a practice that became established in China as Buddhism geographically migrated from India and Nepal to China. It is meditating silently while remaining open to the radiance, the illumination, of the Presence of the Absolute. Silent illumination meditation is mostly associated with the Chinese Chan Buddhist or Japanese Zen Buddhist traditions.

The silent illumination practice effectively involves transforming our awareness to a more unconditioned awareness. In reality, these awarenesses are not two. We appear to separate our personal awareness from unconditioned awareness through the application of conceptual convictions.

The benefit of *shikantaza* is that it assists us in softening the concepts of identification, relaxing perception, and blurring all separation. That is, this meditation begins to gently challenge our beliefs that we are exclusively a separate self whose life success is entirely dependent for survival upon each of our individual actions.

Shikantaza
Meditation Practice

— Either close your eyes or leave them open slightly
with a soft downward gaze. Seating yourself in a
comfortable position, place your hands in your
lap or high on your thighs. Take a few deep-belly
breaths, inhaling and exhaling as thoroughly
as possible. Feel your feet on the ground while
noticing the support of the floor in the building
you are in.

— See if you can feel the support of the earth
beneath you, holding you right in this moment.
Relax any optional tension your body is holding.

— While resting with awareness, sense your inner
field. Is there a distinct perception of mind *and*
body in your experience? Or, in contrast, is the
inner experience a unified body/mind? If you are
feeling a separate mind and a separate body, that
suggests there is a conceptual division between
the two. For most people, this conceptual
conviction separating mind from body is in the
neck area.

— Hold the separate mind, the separate body, and
the conceptual division of the two all at once

with no priority. No need to do anything; just let these perceived separate parts coexist.

- At some point, you will perceive an inner unification of body and mind—a body/mind. When that is present, ever so slightly open your eyes. With a soft downward gaze, perceive your inner and outer atmosphere or energy. Inner energy is contained in the body boundary, and outer energy is outside the body boundary.
- Do you perceive an inside distinct from an outside? If you are perceiving a separate inside and outside, there is usually a conceptual separation of a body or body boundaries. While holding inner, outer, and conceptual separation of a body or body boundaries, let these coexist. Holding all these perceptions in awareness, just breathe.
- In time, the distinct concepts of inner, outer, and conceptual boundary will soften and drop. There will then be a unified, universal, objective wholeness of inner and outer, a unity of Oneness.
- In this unified Oneness of inner and outer, let awareness stretch or open to the totality of your field of awareness. Notice if you can feel any edges, any boundaries, in awareness. Remaining open and with awareness expanded, just be.

Everything, including all aspects of direct experience, is always right here, always.

Everything, including all aspects of direct experience, is always right here, always. The core quality of the universe is hereness, also called thusness or suchness in Buddhism. That means there is nowhere other than right here that we can ever abide. These are the important experiential learnings *shikantaza* affords us. Our connection with awareness in this meditation softens to the point that we can feel what should be an end point to awareness, yet there is no end point. Awareness is vast and without any kind of limitation, end point, or boundary.

My Experience with Shikantaza Meditation

I first came in contact with *shikantaza* in the mid-1970s. I learned about it from one of the first Zen books in English. In those days, new students were initially given breath counting as their meditation. This was a basic concentration-developing meditation. I counted breaths for two years.

After two years, I felt ready for *shikantaza*. I learned *shikantaza* at a Zen center. The monastic teaching guided us through all the physical postures (that is, legs crossed, hands in lap, hands in a concentration position called a mudra, eyes closed halfway). There were absolutely no instructions or comments on the inner experience. I had no idea what to do in the meditation.

I approached a number of seasoned meditators to inquire what they were doing in the meditation. Each senior I asked gave me a different answer. In effect, no one had an idea what to do in *shikantaza* other than assume the physical posture.

When I began to teach about twenty years ago, I uncovered a connection between Theravada traditional meditations and *shikantaza*. Applying some of the technical knowledge I had gained in Theravada Buddhist meditations, I began teaching the three stages of *shikantaza*: (1) unity of inner awareness (unity of body and mind), (2) further unity of awareness (unity of inside the skin and outside the skin), and (3) opening to the unity of our awareness and universal/Absolute awareness.

Shikantaza is still a foundational meditation in my practice. It is a resting in whatever functions or qualities of the Absolute are presenting in any given moment. *Shikantaza* is being the Absolute seamlessly.

"The infinite universe was now my heart"

I have been meditating for many years and over that time have learned to regularly enter samadhi (meditative absorption). This samadhi had the effect of quieting my mind. It also opened the door to *kenshō*, which are direct encounters with the great reality that is always present beyond the ordinary discriminating mind and is referred to as the Absolute.

From the consistent practice of meditation and experiences of *kenshō*, I came to feel the Absolute Presence and dark mystery intimately. Long periods would pass without any troubling sense of self, just a silent internal witnessing of the miraculous arising and passing away. Yet in many meditations, my mind would trigger a reaction of anger about something coming up in my everyday life, and I would have to start the process of letting go again. After much internal examination, it became clear that this core wound had been with me in various forms since my earliest memories and was consistent with known traumas suffered by my family over several generations.

Seeking support, I began a series of guided Absolute meditations with Mugen Sensei, a well-regarded spiritual teacher. I was committing to opening my heart and really facing and relinquishing the fear I was still holding on to. The meditations were powerful and helped open and clear the resistances on physical, psychological, and spiritual levels. The work continued to deepen as I felt an inner energy opening and widening from my heart to the crown of my head and radiating out well beyond the body. My sense of the Absolute Presence grew ever greater, holding me in its embrace for long periods of time.

While things were improving, there was still a subtle edge of tension and some physical pain. One day I decided to visit a massage therapist to help move the physical pain along. As I relaxed into the massage, a deep peacefulness softened both my consciousness and awareness. Very quickly I fell into a deep enveloping silence, barely aware of the therapist working. After some time, I could feel a powerful energy building and radiating through the heart and up past the crown of the head. The therapist said, "I'm being told to just hold space for you." The energy continued to build and radiate intensely, but my mind was dark. Then I saw figures of light whom I recognized as my ancestors. I heard them saying, "All is healed. It's safe to let go. Just let go." A sense of tremendous energy was being released throughout and beyond the physical body. My mind went into the deepest blackness and all sense of time and space ceased. Everything had fallen away.

Eventually awareness returned, but I was not the same. The therapist spoke with a distant voice, saying that I had been out for more than two hours and that the light and energy coming through the body exceeded anything she had ever encountered. She felt her own life had been altered. I felt profound relief and scanned for familiar signs but found the old wounds and attachments that supported a sense of self had vanished. I was left with a gentle, silent radiance that was unmistakable: The infinite universe was now my heart, a heart at peace.

—STUDENT 4

"No need to be anywhere else than just here"

I attended a six-day "Demystifying Awakening" retreat with Mugen Sensei. Some psychological and emotional issues arose during this retreat, as they always seem to do in meditation, and at times when they became too strong, I had to turn my attention toward them, to try and understand and resolve them.

I had not experienced Cessation before, so I was curious and wondered what I needed to work on in order for Cessation to be able to arise. To try and find that out, I at times asked myself about this. I then watched the response, the felt sense in the body as well as any mental or emotional reactions. In meditation, I generally just tried to stay with whatever arose, comfortable or uncomfortable thoughts and feelings, etc.

The second-last day of the retreat I felt a bit tired in the middle of the day, and I decided to rest before going back to the meditation hall. Lying on the bed, I had an impulse to feel or check what was inside. Pity then arose in the stomach area followed by spaciousness and love in the chest area. It felt like there was more bubbling up from within, like there was a momentum that came up all by itself. I got an impulse or longing to let go of personality things like attachments, pride, stubbornness, feelings of superiority and being right, etc. It was a very loving experience. I felt as though I was very tired of these things and that it would just be so very nice to just let them go! When I felt this, there was also a conscious moment where the actual letting go happened, which felt very freeing and wonderful. It was as though all negative things that weighed me down disappeared. I'm not sure how to describe what was left—effortless and loving awareness!

The awareness at this point was probably in the head area, and the wisdom eye seemed to be activated. The felt sense of a body disappeared, and thinking activity stopped, as well as any awareness of all external input through the five senses. Then the internal seeing went all black and deeply calm; everything went very black and completely still. The last thing I remember was that all I knew was stillness and blackness.

After some time, there was a little rush of awareness coming back, and I could again sense the body. For the first time in my life I noticed how much noise there is in a body lying completely still in bed! I could feel the many vibrations, blood rushing around, and other feelings in the body. The mind at this stage was a pure awareness, no thinking about anything in the past or future. There were no worries as to what I should do—all was very well and there were no concerns about survival or any other concerns of what I could or should do. I just was, right here, thoroughly contented!

Directly afterward, I knew something had happened, but I did not really bother about what this phenomenon was, because everything was just very wonderful. There was absolutely no need to try and be anywhere else than just here in this moment. It was a very pristine and comfortable experience, soft, gentle, and lovely. I did not know what this comfortable experience was. After coming back, there was absolutely no gratification or feeling of accomplishment by a me—just a pristine state of mind, all accepting, no clinging or doer whatsoever. In the upcoming interview with my teacher—Mugen Sensei—he confirmed this experience as Cessation.

Afterward I walked in the forest and the only things present were awareness and Presence, nothing else! Well, love was there as well but it was a subtle love (and it was difficult or impossible to distinguish love from awareness and Presence). There was no me and no regard or wondering as to what an I observing actually was. There was no need for memories, not much thinking, no planning the future, only effortlessly being aware and present.

(Some days after this experience, this very subtle and nonhuman way of observing made me feel a bit of aloneness and isolation. Even doubt arose as to whether or not I was on the correct path and if I wanted to continue this path. It felt like a little too cut off from the human parts of me, I guess—a little too transparent and without any substance to a me. Directly after the experience it all felt great though, so these feelings came a few days after.)

The *satori* experience about one month earlier felt more like a lightning bolt hitting, where many things changed at once. The Cessation experience was incredibly soft, pristine, and refined, a tranquil and loving experience that seemed to smooth out the rough parts of the behavior of the personality patterning. There was less of a sense of personality/self after this experience. This resulted in there being fewer trigger mechanisms in daily life. Coming back to society after this retreat was also very easy, like a soft landing.

—STUDENT 3

AUTHOR'S NOTE: The "wisdom eye" is a name used in Theravada Buddhism to describe the functioning of inner seeing or deep intuitive knowing associated with the chakra in the center of the forehead. In the Zen tradition, this is referred to as the "Dharma eye."

CONCLUSION

AS WE DEEPEN and expand our contact with the qualities of our true nature, an awakeness begins to be felt and experienced as a kind of background mind. "Background mind" means the awakeness is operating, running, in the background of our mind always or nearly always. We can feel the truth of the background mind. Our attention is habituated to residing in foreground mind. "Foreground mind" is the mind of thoughts—or self-identity—memory, and history. This is where the sense of self reigns.

There is typically an impatience at this time. We can see the *dukkha*, the unsatisfactoriness and suffering, of the foreground mind of me with all its reactivity, positionality, and historic meaning, while concurrently pining for the background mind with its deep peace and comforting qualities of love and spaciousness.

The way to hold this stage of development is to be as patient as possible and maintain contact with both minds. Let awareness reside in both background and foreground mind without holding a preference for either. Do not reject either. Just be with both.

> *When we can rest in whatever mind is right here, we can have complete freedom.*

With sustained contact with both background and foreground mind, the line separating these two softens and begins to fade. When we are neutral toward either mind, welcoming without clinging or rejection, the line separating these two minds drops. We come to realize that these are simply two functions, two ways, of the Absolute appearing in the world.

When we can rest in whatever mind is right here, we can have complete freedom. Everything is the Absolute. Everything is functioning just as it should in its own truth.

As we move more deeply into the mind of unity, the nondual mind of no subject or object, we have greater ability to fully surrender to the peace and stillness of the Absolute and potentially be absorbed into the source, power, dynamism of the Absolute—Cessation. Cessation is the ceasing of all materiality and mentality. This is a lights-out, direct experience of a potent, dreamless sleep with no consciousness or awareness active.

Experientially, Cessation is a process and realization that begins as awareness and consciousness are deeply drawn into the peace and stillness of the unmanifest Absolute.

It is through the practice of opening to the vast blackness of the unmanifest Absolute that we encounter profound peacefulness and rich stillness. By opening deeper and deeper to this Absence, this no-thing-ness, we loosen our self-concepts, releasing what in us is conditioned, and unfurl awareness into the profound, still peacefulness of the unconditioned Absolute.

As we approach the wholesome inclusion of Cessation, we will see that as awareness and consciousness are drawn deeper into the still peacefulness, our words, our concepts, our thoughts become still. There is still a perspective of awareness, a locus of perception. Slowly, consciousness, awareness with a historic reference, quiets and ceases.

Many people reach this subtle, potent state of no state. This is not yet Cessation as there is a locus, a place, of perception. I call this the "Cessation waiting room."

Abiding in the Cessation waiting room is powerfully transformative. Our perception is a bare perception without thought-concept and without historic referencing. We are in the potency of Cessation as it purifies all concepts and all attachments we have to mentality or materiality.

Finally, when we are sufficiently steeped in the potency of the Cessation waiting room, pure, nonconceptual awareness (that is, awareness that knows exclusively by direct contact) ceases. This is Cessation, a lights-out blackness like a dreamless sleep. There is no awareness, perception, thought, or identity here.

To be in a nondual, silent, merging union with Cessation is profoundly altering, should we have a sustained experience. A Cessation realization that is brief, less than thirty minutes in duration, does not seem to be as deeply impactful as one of thirty minutes or more, based on my observations working with students. This is not to say that a brief merger into pure no-thing-ness is not immeasurably profound in itself.

Only after rousing from Cessation are we impacted by the experience. I sometimes refer to this as leaving home for vacation and returning to find your household furniture more favorably rearranged.

We are truly free when we wake up out of these conceptual positions of mind.

Deeply steeping in the profound Absence, no-thing-ness, of Cessation is life altering. This is the source of all reality. All form and all formlessness emanate from this profound, deep stillness and peacefulness. It accepts everything without preference. Awareness and consciousness stop when merged with Cessation. Cessation is us in this experience. We put down and release all worldly views; all concepts defining us and our reality fall away. We are left with nothing. The Absence of Cessation reboots our belief system. We can no longer hold the false views, conclusions, and opinions of our culture, religion, or family. We are truly free when we wake up out of these conceptual positions of mind.

The Absence of Cessation can become our foundation in the *Daigo-tettei* Awakening. This is the profound Awakening of the Buddhas, of the realized teachers in all faith traditions. Yet all these experiences of aligning directly and truly with ultimate reality are fully available to you, too, beginning right now. Should you feel and hear the call of the Absolute, wordlessly, silently, forcefully beckoning you deeper, here are the practices that will liberate you from your limiting self-definitions and conceptual understandings and convictions—soothing and releasing you with unrestricted ease. Freedom is always right here.

ACKNOWLEDGMENTS

I HUMBLY OFFER deep gratitude to my teachers for their wisdom and integrity in preserving these important teachings and practices and entrusting me as a lineage holder. I am also deeply grateful to my students. Their clarity and dedication are inspiring to me.

A special thank-you to the team who took this book from my first manuscript to the beneficial book it is—Carra Simpson, Erin Parker, Jazmin Welch, Julia Grandison, Lynn Slobogian, and Samuel Quinn.

My deep gratitude to my transmitting Zen teacher Mark Sando Mininberg, Roshi; his transmitting teacher Tetsugan Glassman, Roshi; and his transmitting teacher Taizan Maezumi, Roshi. I felt and feel the potency of the lineage realization as I offer these teachings.

APPENDIX

Bodhidharma's One-Mind Precepts and the Four Bodhisattva Vows

By Stephen Mugen Snyder, Sensei

Precept of Atonement

All past and present karma,
Born from beginningless greed, hate, and delusion,
Born of my body, speech, and mind,
I now fully atone.

Precepts of Refuge

I take refuge in the Buddha.
I take refuge in the Dharma.
I take refuge in the Saṅgha.

Three Pure Precepts

Cease from evil.
Do only good.
Do good for others.

Ten Precepts

The Absolute is subtle and mysterious. In the realm of the pure unconditioned, cherishing life is called the **Precept of Preciousness**.

The Absolute is subtle and mysterious. In the realm of the pure unconditioned, being content with our material and spiritual possessions is called the **Precept of Contentment**.

The Absolute is subtle and mysterious. In the realm of the pure unconditioned, exercising appropriate intimacy is called the **Precept of Respect**.

The Absolute is subtle and mysterious. In the realm of the pure unconditioned, speaking sincerely is called the **Precept of Truth**.

The Absolute is subtle and mysterious. In the realm of the pure unconditioned, preserving a wholesome mind is called the **Precept of Clarity**.

The Absolute is subtle and mysterious. In the realm of the pure unconditioned, offering respect to all is called the **Precept of Honor**.

The Absolute is subtle and mysterious. In the realm of the pure unconditioned, honoring the profound uniqueness of each being is called the **Precept of Equity**.

The Absolute is subtle and mysterious. In the realm of the pure unconditioned, offering appropriate support is called the **Precept of Generosity**.

The Absolute is subtle and mysterious. In the realm of the pure unconditioned, maintaining heartfelt compassion is called the **Precept of Strength**.

The Absolute is subtle and mysterious. In the realm of the pure unconditioned, respecting all beings exactly as they are is called the **Precept of the Three Treasures**.

Four Bodhisattva Vows

Sentient beings are numberless; I vow to save them.
Desires are inexhaustible; I vow to put an end to them.
The Dharmas are boundless; I vow to master them.
The Buddha Way is unattainable; I vow to attain it.

GLOSSARY

Absence: A synonym for emptiness in Buddhism. It is a quality of reality where there is nothing apparent to ordinary perception, yet something substantial and significant is present and perceived intuitively, directly through experiential contact.

absence of self: The experience of the customary self-identity being increasingly transparent and difficult to locate within.

Absolute: The source of all life animation and manifestation of all form and formless reality.

Absolute realm: The realm where the Absolute can be directly and deeply perceived, experienced, and merged with. The Absolute can function as unmanifest or manifest. The unmanifest is characterized by dark blackness, Absence (emptiness), deep peace, and profound stillness. The manifest, on the other hand, appears as a brilliant brightness of purity, pure unconditioned love, pure Presence (Beingness), and pure awareness (awareness without historical references).

accordion effect: Whenever awareness expands to a new level, the self-identity generally reacts shortly thereafter by briefly contracting as tightly as is possible.

ānāpānasati: See breath awareness meditation.

authentic: A description of something that originates directly in the unconditioned Absolute.

Awakening and First Awakening: The Absolute awakening to itself from the dream of solely being a separate me. Awakening is an experience in which the sense of self becomes transparent to our self-perception, we are deeply experiencing the undivided nondual love of the Absolute, and we have the aha moment of recognizing that no-self and unity are our true identity. First Awakening is an experience that contains (1) a deep experience of absence of self, (2) clear seeing of one's true nature as one's true identity, and (3) a thorough unity experience where all is One, or everything is a fabric of Oneness.

awareness: Perception, with or without consciousness, of internal and external events unfolding.

background mind and **foreground mind**: Background mind is where awakeness is operating always, or nearly always in the background of perceptions. Foreground mind is the mind of thoughts, or self-identity, and memory and history. This is where the sense of self reigns. These are perceived as separate after a First Awakening. With deepening practice these begin to wholesomely integrate.

Beingness: Unconditioned Presence.

brahmavihāras: Ancient Buddhist heart meditations that open our awareness to unconditioned qualities of our true nature such as equanimity (*upekkhā*), empathetic joy (*muditā*), compassion (*karuṇā*), unconditioned love (*mettā*), and innate goodness, to name a few.

breath awareness meditation: Called *ānāpānasati* from the Pali *ānāpāna* (breath) and *sati* (awareness). Typically, the first meditation given to new Theravada Buddhist students by the Buddha. This practice concentrates and purifies the mind through turning away from the habituated thinking and routine concepts. This practice can lead to the deepest level of meditative concentration called *jhāna*. (Please see my book *Practicing the Jhānas* for details on this practice.)

Cessation: The experience of complete merging into the pristine stillness and the unmeasurable depth of peace and the rich Absence (emptiness) of the unmanifest Absolute, in which all mentality and materiality cease. Another name for a potential enlightenment experience, as there will be experiential changes following Cessation that permanently change the self-identity, including an Awakening experience. Also known as *nirodha.*

Cessation waiting room: My term to describe the experience when awareness is hovering on the cusp of Cessation but not fully absorbed with Cessation. Many of the benefits of Cessation can be experienced while we develop greater trust in absorption with Cessation.

Chan: The Chinese Buddhist tradition of using *kōan* and *shikantaza* (silent illumination meditation) to open and directly experience Cessation and likely a *kenshō*, an Awakening experience.

concentration meditation: A collection of meditations in which the meditator stays with one meditative object, prioritizing it over all other sense data or experience.

conceptual knowing and **nonconceptual knowing**: Conceptual knowing is when we compare a present experience with our memories of prior life experiences. Nonconceptual knowing is direct knowing without comparing the present direct memory with our history.

consciousness: Awareness coupled with ordinary and intuitive knowing.

core wound: The inner experience of instability or the perception of weakness often found in the solar plexus area of our body, also known in psychological terms as "core egoic deficiency."

Daigo-tettei: The third level of Awakening experience (*kenshō*) in the Zen tradition, in which the self-identity drops away and is not reactivated again.

defilements: The Buddhist defilements are core pieces of every egoic structure and self-identity. The defilements are (1) desire or greed, (2) aversion or ill will, and (3) delusion. It is understood that while everyone has all three of these defilements, we each have an inherent proclivity for being predominantly a desire or an aversion type.

Dharma: Teaching or universal law. Also known as Dhamma.

dual unity: A state where the infant is in an undifferentiated state of individuation and is thus in a nondual union with all other beings until the self-identity lands in the individual consciousness.

dukkha: The first noble truth of Buddhism that human life contains unsatisfactoriness or suffering.

eternal now: The true measure of time. The past and future are concepts only. The present moment is the only unit of time and experience.

felt sense: Intuitive perception of what is not visually apparent.

first arrow and **second arrow**: Concepts the Buddha used in his teaching. The first arrow is pain or initial discomfort. The second arrow is the commentary, story, or resistance to the first arrow.

the good, pure, innocent one: A psychological structure formed early in life to elevate the hierarchical position of our caregivers as well as create a persona that does no wrong. If we are the innocent, pure one there is no basis for the caregiver to withhold love or support in any form.

hara: Area in the belly about two fingerbreadths below the navel and about two to three fingerbreadths beneath the surface of the skin. It is an energy center, called a "chakra" in the Yogic tradition. It is an important inner seat of the Absolute that is primarily nonconceptual.

innate goodness: The inherent quality of our true nature; goodness not dependent on any manner of doing or way of being.

jhāna: The third level of concentration, also called absorption concentration; a nondual state with complete awareness, no thoughts, and no discernible self.

jhāna **factors**: Available in all meditations; (1) applied awareness (*vitakka*), (2) sustained awareness (*vicāra*), (3) joy (*pīti*), (4) bliss (*sukha*), and (5) one-pointedness (*ekaggatā*).

karma: A complex compilation of all past experiences into present-moment reality. In other words, whatever we have done in the past conditions our perception of this moment. Engaging actively with meditation or spiritual practices helps dissolve past karma.

karuṇā: Compassion, a kindhearted holding that allows us, and others, to be with our pain and persevere. An unconditioned quality of our true nature.

kasina: A mind-made, disklike object that can be perceived meditatively by either visual or felt-sense contact. There are color *kasinas*, four element *kasinas* (earth, water, fire, and air), and two very subtle *kasinas*, light *kasina* and space *kasina*.

kenshō: Seeing into one's true nature; from the Zen tradition's map of Awakening.

kōan: A spiritual paradox that cannot be resolved by the thinking mind; spiritual intuition and realization offer the perfect solution.

levels of concentration: (1) Momentary concentration, (2) access concentration, and (3) absorption concentration (*jhāna*).

mettā: Usually translated as "loving-kindness"; the unconditioned love of the Absolute.

misattunement: When our caregivers attend to us. They are operating from prior experience as well as from their self-definition of a me. The intent may be clear, but the dysfunctions in operation color the purity of the original intent to care for another.

muditā: Empathetic joy, or the joy we feel at another's success, happiness, or joy. Literally their joy or success feels indistinguishable from our joy or success. An unconditioned quality of our true nature.

mudra: Positioning of the hands in meditation. A mudra is an energy posture that evokes particular energies of the Absolute.

narcissism: The elevation of the perception of a me, a self, over others. Our deep, shadowed feelings of worthlessness or inferiority drive our need to be seen in a particular light or with a particular lens by another.

Nibbāna: An experience of Cessation in which all materiality and mentality cease. Also known as *nirvāṇa*.

nimitta: A mind-made product of deep concentration meditation on an unchanging meditative object.

nondual state: A perception in which one's consciousness is experienced as an undivided unity with all of life, a completeness with no remainders or exclusions.

no-self: An experience in which the customary self-identity is absent (or transparent) and a unity experience of all is One is concurrently present.

off-the-cushion meditation and **on-the-cushion meditation**: Refers to the importance of continuity. For a meditation to reach its depths of experience we need to maintain ongoing contact when seated in formal meditation as well as while maneuvering in our life.

Oneness: The function of the Absolute and all universes is a unified, indivisible unity.

particular realm (formless *jhāna*): The world can be viewed as being comprised of form (tangible structure) and formless (no discernible structure). In the deep concentration of breath awareness meditation, we can merge into profound qualities of the Absolute such as boundless space, boundless consciousness, boundless no-thing-ness, and neither perception nor non-perception. The experience of merging with these qualities is known as entering the particular realm.

Presence: Experiential contact with the Beingness quality of this present moment.

proactive effort: Affirmative doingness, used when we must initiate action or behavior.

receptive effort: Appropriate and timely minimizing or surrendering of personal effort, which we shift to when pro-active effort starts to work.

resistances: Psychological or emotional patterns of mind or behavior that restrict awareness from contacting qualities of our true nature, including a First Awakening.

samadhi: Very deep concentration meditation. Samadhi would be referring to either access concentration or absorption concentration (*jhāna*).

samatha: Another term for the purification-of-mind practices in Theravada Buddhism that teach the student to focus on one meditative object at a time, to unify awareness while balancing energy and meditative concentration; *samatha* translates as concentration, serenity, or tranquility.

Saṅgha: A community of Buddhist practitioners. This can mean those gathered for a specific retreat or practice place, or students of a particular teacher. Saṅgha is a refuge for each of us when we feel adrift in our life or spiritual practice.

satori: The sustained *kenshō* experience of seeing into one's true nature. In *satori*, the experience is both more far-reaching and more sustaining than in *kenshō*. *Satori* will awaken in 51 percent or more of consciousness for a shift in identity from the customary personality view to true nature.

self-identity: The psychological patterns of mind and behavior that define who we are to ourselves; self-concept; self-recognition.

shadow material: The psychological identity that is unseen and unconscious. It operates under our inner radar of perception.

shikantaza: The Japanese name for silent illumination meditation.

silent illumination meditation: The Chinese Chan Buddhist meditation of bringing awareness to unify (1) body/mind, (2) inside/outside, and (3) vastness without conceptual boundaries.

source: The Absolute; the origin of all creation and manifestation. Cessation is the origin of the Absolute.

spiritual bypass: Orienting exclusively to transcendent, blissful, joyful experiences whenever we are confronted with difficult or unpleasant emotional states.

suchness: The Zen expression of true reality, "not two, not one"; the realization that duality is a position of mind. It is resting in and abiding with the Absolute without separation or division. Also called thusness.

superego: A psychological structure where we activate the presence of a parent or caregiver within to help guide us and to have them near.

suttas: The Pali term for a sermon or religious talk offered by Shakyamuni Buddha; known as *sutras* in Sanskrit.

Theravada Buddhism: The tradition of Buddhism maintaining the traditional meditative practices of the Buddha.

thought-concept: The concepts and ideas we construct, and the mentalizing we perform, in an attempt to define and control our inner and outer world.

thought-emotion: Emotion that has a quality of "me" embedded in it.

true nature: The true, core foundation of unconditioned reality. This refers to qualities of the Absolute embedded in our particular consciousness.

upekkhā: Equanimity, a feeling of perfect balance. Everything that is occurring inside or outside of us is exactly right in this moment. An unconditioned quality of our true nature.

wisdom eye: The functioning of inner seeing or deep intuitive knowing associated with the chakra in the center of the forehead. In the Zen tradition, this is referred to as the "Dharma eye."

Zen Buddhism: The Buddhist tradition evolving from Chinese Chan Buddhism, in which Awakening is the primary objective.

ABOUT THE AUTHOR

Stephen Mugen Snyder, Sensei, began practicing daily meditation in 1976. Since then, he has studied Buddhism extensively—investigating and engaging in Zen, Tibetan, Theravada, and Western nondual traditions. He was authorized to teach in the Theravada Buddhist tradition in 2007 and in the Zen Buddhist schools of Sōtō and Rinzai in 2022. Stephen is a senior student of Mark Sando Mininberg, Roshi, and a transmitted teacher in the White Plum Asanga—the body of teachers in the Maezumi Roshi lineage.

Stephen's resonant and warmhearted teaching style engages students around the globe through in-person and online retreats, as well as one-on-one coaching. He encourages students to turn toward their true nature and, with realization of their true nature, embody their true identity. Stephen is the author of four books, including *Trust in Awakening, Demystifying Awakening,* and *Buddha's Heart.* He also coauthored *Practicing the Jhānas.* For more information, please visit awakeningdharma.org.

DID YOU BENEFIT FROM
LIBERATING THE SELF?

SHARE YOUR PRAISE

Did this book offer new insights into Buddhist teachings that are benefiting your daily life or interactions? If so, a review shared through your favorite online retailer would be warmly welcomed. A few minutes of your time could help others find this book and benefit as you have.

PLACE A BULK ORDER

Would you like to share this book with a group or a class? Please be in touch! We can offer bulk discounts for orders of ten or more copies to most locations. Please write to hello@awakeningdharma.org.

KEEP IN TOUCH

For more about Stephen's books, workshops, and other offerings, please visit awakeningdharma.org.

ALSO BY STEPHEN SNYDER

*Trust in Awakening: A Zen Teaching
on Accessing the Absolute*
PAPERBACK • 978-1-7347810-7-6 • $14.95
E-BOOK • 978-1-7347810-8-3 • $9.95
PUBLISHED SEPTEMBER 2022

A fresh and powerful reworking of the seventh-
century Zen poem, the *Xin Xin Ming*. This
poem has guided and inspired serious Zen practitioners on the
path to Awakening for centuries. Structuring its stanzas in *kōan*-like
meditations, Snyder interprets the poem's directions to seeing the
Absolute, the source, fully manifesting in each of us—to Awakening.

*Demystifying Awakening: A Buddhist Path
of Realization, Embodiment, and Freedom*
HARDCOVER • 978-1-7347810-6-9 • $24.95
PAPERBACK • 978-1-7347810-4-5 • $16.95
E-BOOK • 978-1-7347810-5-2 • $9.95
PUBLISHED MARCH 2022

A practice path in the process of Awakening—
in this lifetime. *Demystifying Awakening* clearly explains experiences of Awakening, highlighting the natural resistances and how
to work with them; outlines steps for developing a wholesome
livelihood: the natural embodiment of realization; and offers
extensive meditations and practices that support each step on
the path.

*Buddha's Heart: Meditation Practice for
Developing Well-Being, Love, and Empathy*
PAPERBACK • 978-1-7347810-2-1 • $16.95
E-BOOK • 978-1-7347810-3-8 • $9.95
PUBLISHED NOVEMBER 2020

An original and clear path to the powerful *brahmavihāras*—ancient Buddhist heart practices. These practices offer rich, soothing support for the soul and a portal to spiritual awakening and deepening self-realization. *Buddha's Heart* teaches what seems counterintuitive but is undeniably true: the more we open our hearts, the more resilient and flexible we are. And the more authentically vulnerable we are, the safer and more protected we become.

*Stress Reduction for Lawyers, Law Students,
and Legal Professionals: Learning to Relax*
PAPERBACK • 978-1-7347810-0-7 • $14.95
E-BOOK • 978-1-7347810-1-4 • $9.95
PUBLISHED SEPTEMBER 2020

A practical guide for a more relaxed and enjoyable legal career—authored by a retired lawyer and senior meditation teacher. This book offers straightforward techniques to identify the events that cause stress in your work, apply practices that support deep relaxation, and develop greater satisfaction in your work and personal life.

*Practicing the Jhānas: Traditional
Concentration Meditation as Presented
by the Venerable Pa Auk Sayadaw*

PAPERBACK • 978-1-59030-733-5 • $22.95

E-BOOK • 978-0-8348-2282-5 • $17.99

PUBLISHED DECEMBER 2009

COAUTHORED WITH TINA RASMUSSEN

A clear and in-depth presentation of the traditional Theravada concentration meditation known as *jhāna* practice, developed from practicing *jhāna* meditation in retreat under the guidance of one of the great living meditation masters, the Venerable Pa Auk Sayadaw.

www.ingramcontent.com/pod-product-compliance
Lightning Source LLC
Chambersburg PA
CBHW021221130626
46554CB00004B/1311